THEORIES: SIZE 12

Laugh!
You know you want to.

Jody Dyer

Crippled Beagle Publishing

This book is protected under the copyright laws of the United States of America. Any reproduction or unauthorized use in print or digital format is prohibited without express permission of the author except brief quotes for use in interviews, newspaper or magazine articles, or reviews.

Copyright ©2016 Crippled Beagle Publishing
Knoxville, Tennessee

Cover concept by Debbie Boles
Cover design and artwork by Mary Balas
Photo credits: Jody Dyer

Special thanks for the time and talents of retired English teacher Donna Cantrell, writer and editor Linda Albert, and poet, writer, and editor Christina Drill.

Second Edition ISBN-13: 978-1-7321555-5-8

For interviews, excerpts for reviews, or information, contact the author. dyer.cbpublishing@gmail.com

For the Owl Squad and the Kings, Hot Sox,
and Irish mamas—my sisters in Christ and comedy.

Theories

Preface 1
Theory 1: People write diaries hoping someone else will read them. 5
Theory 2: Anyone can learn from anyone. 8
Theory 3: Teachers are the most entertaining people on the planet. 14
Theory 4: The only thing worse than teacher fashion is *substitute* teacher fashion. 21
Theory 5: You should be nice to everyone you meet because you *will* meet again, *especially* if you weren't nice in the first place. 27
Theory 6: Don't judge a woman by her accent or her breast size. 31
Theory 7: Play a sport. Even if you suck at it. 35
Theory 8: If you want the ultimate college experience, join the band. ... 43
Theory 9: Everyone should work in a restaurant. 51
Theory 10: In youth sports, parents are the real performers. 62
Theory 11: The more a zoo advertises a critter, the less likely visitors are to actually see that critter. 70
Theory 12: Bicycle guys are selfish & make other people late for work. 75
Theory 13: As people get old, they morph into the opposite sex. 80
Theory 14: Humans try to force things to be what things cannot be. 89
Theory 15: Tailgate etiquette is *not* an oxymoron. 98
Theory 16: Think you can do somebody else's job? Wrong, chicken lips! 110
Theory 17: Funerals beat weddings, for guests anyway. 128
Theory 18: Blind dates are the best dates ever! 146
Theory 19: All mothers need sister wives. 155
Theory 20: Never call a woman fat, lazy, or selfish. Them's fightin' words. 164

"Against the assault of laughter nothing can stand."
—Mark Twain, *The Mysterious Stranger*

Preface

Think back to your earliest academic accomplishment. Did it involve mastery of a toy? How about completion of a dot-to-dot worksheet, or better yet, completion of an *invisible ink* dot-to-dot worksheet? Surely you didn't move the stickers on your cousin's Rubik's Cube. Hopefully, your first great mind-teasing success was genuine. Mine was just that—genuine. And simple. My first memorable moment of personal pride and parental praise occurred when I wrote my name, letters in accurate order, for the first time. I lived in Pigeon Forge in East Tennessee. I put the then-damaging, fat Crayola magic marker to a "ditto." I bore down so hard the ink likely bled through the ditto onto our tan corduroy ottoman. I wrote my name. J – O – D – Y. My one-of-a-kind mother, known here as "Delicious," applauded in her typically exuberant fashion (she's notorious for being the first and last audience member to clap, regardless of the performance) and demanded that my precious daddy, known here as "Pooh," verbalize his admiration, too.

Another favorite memory occurred when Mrs. Wear, my fifth-grade teacher, said, "Jody, you are so witty." I looked that word up in *Webster's Dictionary* and was quite pleased with my new label. In middle school, my teachers and Delicious urged me to enter essay contests. They said I had a gift with words. By this time, I was addicted to praise.

My high school's girls' basketball coach called me Tongue-Lasher" for my fearless verbal defense tactics and attempts at humor. I don't think I was mean. I hated, and still hate, snobs.

I was uninhibited. Yeah, that's the term: ***uninhibited***. All high-schoolers should feel so free! I'm known in my parts (and for my parts --- more on that later) for saying what everyone else is thinking. I admit it. I love attention and praise. I also love WORDS; I love to write. I especially love to torture myself by trying to write humor, which, in my experience, is the toughest genre to master.

Humor can be hurtful. I can think some pretty mean, tongue-lashing thoughts. I'm bold, especially when speaking through a desktop keyboard. I could certainly make you laugh if I didn't have this burden we call a conscience. Here's the catch. I am a Christian. I am a grown-up. I am a professional. I am a wife, daughter, mother, in-law, friend, cousin, and co-worker. I'd hate to ink myself into solitary social confinement. So, my mature, forty-something goal is to write beyond my teenage tongue-lashing of boys who didn't ask me out because I proclaimed virginity throughout the hallways of Gatlinburg-Pittman High School. I've matured beyond interjecting biting one-liners to clusters of snooty girls.

My goal as a writer is to encourage, enlighten, and entertain. I have written since I was old enough to put words together — sometimes in secret, sometimes for scholarships, sometimes for others, sometimes for my church or employer — but in 2013 I penned a contemporary memoir after enduring a life-altering and life-affirming education. I published *The Eye of Adoption: A Turbulent True Story of Heartache, Humor, & Hope* after an eight-year journey through infertility treatments and the domestic open adoption process. Inspired by the grace and sacrifice of loving birth parents, I felt compelled to help other families touched by adoption. The writing, editing, publishing, and marketing processes were another education, a window into a new industry full of artistic talent and uninhibited writers. I knew it would be pretty cool to see my work bound in a print book in a bookstore and for sale on Amazon and Kindle. I had no idea how spiritual, how fulfilling, and how much fun it would be to make connections with other authors. I *really* had no idea how absolutely awesome it would be to talk with readers through my work, blogs, e-mail, and website. What a trip!

So, reader, let's take a trip together, shall we? I'm an only child who grew up in a picturesque yet isolated "holler" on The Crippled Beagle Farm, named such in honor of two beagles: Joe, who had recovered from a tangle with a vehicle, and Belle, who had backward knees. YES. Backward knees. Mama now has three-legged Waldo, a walker hound who got run over before he was neutered and required a $1,000 amputation. I suppose the farm name was prophetic, since her neighbor-niece also had a three-legged dog named Wiggles. For my urban/suburban friends, a holler is a small valley flanked by hills. Think "Coal Miner's Daughter." Picture a chaw-spittin' cover-all sportin' farmers' co-op customer saying to another, "Yes ma'am. I know them Cantrells. They live in the holler up on Kellum Creek." Having grown up the only child on 72 acres, now, as an unrestricted adult, I can't have enough friends. I love to socialize in person, in writing, and on social media. I'm fascinated by the individual quirks, gifts, or weaknesses I see in people, and I love to share mine. We all have something to teach and to learn. We shouldn't apologize for who we are, as long as we are nice. My editor says I have a thick accent on paper. Good. I want you to KNOW me and see me as a friend on every page, especially those of you who may be lonely, may be frustrated, may be bored, or may just need a laugh.

Throughout my Theories, I nickname the people in my life. Some folks came into my life with tags. Some, I tagged. I am extremely particular about the nicknames, so a few of my very best friends may NOT be nicknamed…yet. I can't just slap a weakly-coined label on someone. That dog won't hunt. Nope. Humor is all about timing. Good nicknames stick. So, if you are one of my best friends and don't have a nickname, that just means I simply care too much about you to grant you anything less than a perfectly sticky nickname that may haunt and "hunt" you for years to come. Also, if I don't mention you in this collection, think one of two things: *Halle-freakin-lu-jah* or *Didn't Jody say she has more Theories to publish? Gulp.*

My friends begged for this book. After I published *The Eye of Adoption*, I related my buddies' pleas to my first book's editor, nicknamed here "Festival of Lights" for her creativity, personality, and colorful writing. I also explained to her that readers were asking, "Dyer, where is your blog?"

I was a full-time teacher working on my master's degree. Sharky was eleven. Gnome was three. Tall Child was 50 (yep, not a typo). I was busy. I griped that I wasn't sure I could manage a blog, and I would rather write the "funny book" as my friends called it. Festival of Lights advised, "Why don't you write the funny book one chapter a week through a blog?"

That's why you hire editors, folks; they are so stinking word-efficient. Amen! Crisis solved. Readers got their blog, buddies get their funny book. Plus, the posts and social media links allowed me to collect funny feedback from followers, much of which I include in all my work.

Some Theories are longer than others. The joy of being a creative person who is also over forty is that I don't care about some ridiculous publishing standard that has an equal word count in every chapter. That's crazy. Some Theories are more profound than others. Some stuff is just funnier than other stuff. Writers write because they love to write, NOT because they love to please. Bear that in mind. Think about it this way: most people HATE to write papers for school, but writers assign themselves eighty-thousand-word papers. The joy in the task is the *freedom* in the task. I don't give a flip what some publishing house I've never met says. Their goal: make money. My goal: laugh and make other people laugh. And think.

So, what's *Theories: Size 12* all about? I wrote one Theory per week for one entire year. Some fancy person once said something like "There's truth in all humor and humor in all truth." My Theories relate just that—truth with humor, humor with truth. You will either find yourself on these pages and agree with my Theories, or you will think *this writer is nuts*. Either way, I hope you at least laugh and feel like you have a new buddy—me! Just call me "Bug." All my friends do.

This peacock loves to show off his tail feathers as he wanders The Crippled Beagle Farm.

Theory 1: People write diaries hoping someone else will read them.

I hope to offer more *purpose* than *personal*, so please forgive me as I talk about my family and myself a little in Theory 1. We'll get the introductions out of the way, then we can move on to more engaging topics.

My father nicknamed me "Bug" because I routinely tossed the clunky airplane-style seatbelt to the side in the backseat of my parents' old Impala, stood, leaned into the front seat, stuck my head right between my parents, and chattered. Constantly. I "bugged them to death." Yes, I talk. All the time. And, I'm direct. Let's just get this over with: I am in my forties and rapidly become a square (physically, not figuratively). I stand five-feet-five inches tall and toggle between 150 and 175 pounds. I'm 150 in the summer because I burn extra calories weeding my yard and trimming my hedges. Actually, my good friend Motor Boater (admired for patiently teaching his boys' friends to tube, ski, and wakeboard on Norris Lake) marvels at my boxwoods. Every spring, when I make the first cut, I text him a photo of me holding my giant electric trimmers. Don't you love tradition? Anyway, when football season starts, I fatten up with water-retaining tailgate delicacies like sausage balls and Rotel and festive beverages — like, well, vodka. I stay thick through the holidays to keep warm and because it is just plain rude to refuse a sweet treat brought to me by a client or student (In addition to documenting the perplexities of the human condition, I ghostwrite, edit, and freelance for folks all over the USA and tutor local teenagers). Each spring, I pull that dang Land's End catalog featuring over-promising, under-delivering swimsuits for big-breasted women out of the mailbox and panic. I cut out carbs and start working in my yard, and the cycle starts again. I wear a size 12. Always have. Probably always will. It's the most common size for middle-aged American women. We can relate, right? Thus, the title of this book, Theories*: Size 12*.

    My mother nicknamed my husband "Tall Child" because, honestly, he's a perpetual teenager. That means he's lots of fun, until it's time to install gutters, complete insurance paperwork, or discipline a child. In all those situations, he prefers to laugh, commend me for my expertise in that particular matter, or bribe with donuts (which he buys in bulk from the local Pilot gas station). The bribees? Our two boys, Sharky and Gnome.

    Our older son is fourteen. His old baseball coach nicknamed him "Sharky" because he is "all cartilage" and he zigzagged down the baselines with odd, yet athletic fluidity. The nickname also fits because Sharky had to move like Michael Phelps on "Wipeout" to navigate the gauntlet of my reproductive system. His very conception and gestation are medically unexplained.

    Tall Child and I also have a five-year-old son, a gift from God and his sweet birth family. I call him The Roaming Gnome because he works a room like he's good-looking, thirty, and single at a cocktail party. In the 44th percentile in height, and 35th percentile in weight, he's no bigger than a minute. He can tighten into a ball like a Roly Poly bug and roll from one end of our front yard to the other. He's like a Yorkshire terrier; he's growing but may always look like a puppy. And, we often have to call him from great distances and dangle treats to lure him inside.

A few summers ago, my nieces, Balloon Girl and Cake, came to visit us. Balloon Girl and Sharky were eight-years-old. Sharky teased Balloon Girl in typical cousin fashion. He hurt her feelings. She retreated to the guest bedroom, and wrote in her diary, "When I first came to Knoxville, I thought I would have a good time, but [Sharky] is being mean." Then, she stomped into the living room, opened the book at Sharky, and demanded, "Here [Sharky], read what I wrote about you in my diary!"

Regardless of genre, writers write to vent, inform, heal, and amuse. I will be completely honest; I hope to do all those things. But, though I write from *my* middle-aged female perspective, I promise my focus is on you. I suffer from secondary infertility, anxiety, a clotting disorder, and working mother guilt. Writing and reading are therapeutic activities. I hope you find healing here. Like you, I've endured my share of struggles, heartaches, and frustrations. I hope you find validation here. I'm a former public-school teacher and intermittent, unfortunate (visiting), retail banking manager—more on that ridiculousness later; it's in my nature to explain things. I hope you learn here. Most of all, I crave laughter like a junior leaguer shakes for Chardonnay at 5:15 p.m. and a Georgia fan demands barbecue at a tailgate. I am a humorist at heart. I hope you laugh here.

On a Smoky mountain hike, Balloon Girl asked, "Aunt Bug, did you bring us here because this is your old school?"

Theory 2: Anyone can learn from anyone.

Delicious taught grade twelve English for almost forty years. She proclaims the number one learning disability in America is not ADHD. It's DNA. She also says that teenagers get a bad rep but are actually loving, lively, tolerant, and compassionate. I taught junior high school for five years, so I agree. Plus, teenagers are FUNNY. We aren't all created with equal academic ability, but enlightened, positive educators like my mother know that every student can learn. They also believe that every student has something to teach others. Even though the Internet is blocked, the doors are bolted, and teachers are vetted through drug and background checks, schools are the most *open* buildings in society. The shielded environment actually creates a bubble in which teachers and students share a unique bond of trust, candid communication, and, in the right environment, good times. Parents, be careful what you say and do at home; students tell trusted teachers everything. Heck, when I was a freshly freckled four-year-old, I told my daycare teacher, "My mama and daddy take showers together."

On that same mature note, I think back to my mother's classroom, where she admonished her school newspaper staff for "talking about dirty stuff." A beautiful junior from the rural area of Catons Chapel said in her tinny East Tennessee twang, "Oh, Mrs. Delicious, youns teachers gotta lighten up. *Ever*body's got a sex life!"

To capstone my post-baccalaureate secondary education certification courses, I performed an eighteen-week student-teaching stretch at Powell High School. The community and school were tight, particularly during football season. Students showed minimal interest in advanced placement courses but filled vocational classrooms. Fights? Weekly. The band (go band!) hosted pep rallies at 7:30 a.m. every football Friday. I operated under two mentors. The first, a typing teacher, taught me all about easy, inexpensive, charity-themed school attire. She loved to read for pleasure. At school. We'll call her *The Giver*. *The Giver* gave me a binder of one semester's worth of lesson plans. My second mentor, let's call her QuickBooks, was a desktop publishing instructor. She was petite, fast, cute, and neat, like a hummingbird. She was a consummate professional *and* grandmother. I was ambitious and had just adopted Gnome. She knew I wanted to do a good job, but she sympathized with my sleep-deprivation, as Gnome was only three months old when I started student teaching. She taught me about collegial etiquette, such as, "Don't ever let football players eat lunch in your computer lab; they'll break something or look at pornography," and, "If you hustle and write to win the grant for four color ink cartridges, hide them from the teachers who did NOT hustle to win the grant." I love to write. I think porn is grotesque. I'm a hustler. We got along well.

QuickBooks and *The Giver* granted me solid instruction, but, hands down, I learned my greatest lessons from their students. The television show "Glee" was a hit because it reflected the drama of high school reality. Students *do* break out into song. Delicious substitute teaches at Sevier County High School (SCHS), which is the arch nemesis to my alma mater, Gatlinburg-Pittman High School (G-P).

When retired Delicious told me she signed up to fill in at SCHS, I asked her, "Why did you choose *that school*?"

She answered, "I was old. I needed the money."

The truth is that it's closer to her home, The Crippled Beagle Farm. Subbing closer to home meant she'd spend less of the insulting payout on gas.

Anyway, one day while Delicious monitored a class at SCHS, for no logical reason, an 11th grade boy began singing Toby Keith's "Red Solo Cup." What happened next? The other students joined in. Think back to your days in school. What memories stand out like buoys in an ocean of worksheets? Off the cuff, ad lib, moments of vulnerability, humor, and play? I think teachers dislike the new evaluation models and federal mandates because they take individuality out of the job. Teachers are scientific artists. They need autonomy, creative freedom, and time. So, you may ask, was Delicious upset when the entire class bellowed "Red Solo Cup"? Yes. She was furious, because she didn't know the words.

Real teachers get it.

Real teachers sing along.

As a student-teacher, I quickly realized that teenagers are so entertaining that I needed to record their remarks. Every day of my teaching career, I carried a composition book with me. Perhaps stopping class to write down teenage quotes wasn't super professional, but, boy, am I glad I did. Anyone can learn from anyone.

I hope you learn from the following sampling from Mrs. Bug's Teenage Quotation Book. I changed students' names to protect their privacy and my earring collection.

Teenage proverbs and revelations

High school boys are not attracted to girls who smoke. Wilson explained, **"Man, soon as I see a hot girl cough up tar, I'm done wit' her."**

The future of the medical industry is sketchy. Shelley, who plans to be a nurse, announced, **"I had strep throat but I'm not airborne anymore."**

Jonie said, **"I will be in college 15 years to be an ob/gyn, but the last four years are residential."**

American teenagers have unique interpretations of race. Charles questioned, **"I don't know why my last name is Rodriguez. I'm American Indian."**

Wilson declared, **"Mrs. Dyer, we can all be ghetto sometimes, even white people."**

Teenagers are romantic and see the real beauty in others. Mama C— *the* regular sub at the school—growls instructions like she starts every day with black coffee, a sausage biscuit, and a pack of unfiltered cigarettes. I watched her, repeatedly, scold Derron, a spastic junior. His reply: **"Oh, Mama C, you know I make you want to be young again!"**

Teenagers are spiritual. Felina told me, **"My grandma is in heaven. My grandpa is in Louisiana."**

Teenagers interpret their parents' behavior in a literal sense. After discussing his ADHD diagnosis, John disclosed, **"My mom has a screaming disorder."**

Despite what you hear, teenagers do have a moral code. This is an exact transcript of a real conversation I had with seventh grader, R'Shawna. By the way, that's not an apostrophe. R'Shawna told me her name is spelled, "R – comma to the top – S H A W N A."

R'Shawna: "Miss D., did you know my brother had a baby when he was 15?"

Me: "No, I didn't. I imagine that was really tough at such a young age. I hope you'll make better decisions."

R'Shawna: "Don't you worry 'bout me, Miss D. I'm a *virgin*."

Me: "Well, that's good, because you are twelve years old."

R'Shawna: "Thas right! And I'm gonna stay a virgin til I gets married. But when I do gets married, I'm gonna bang, bang, bang like a choo-choo train."

My student-teaching experience confirmed that I was meant to be a teacher. Not because I love to learn, write, research, explain, and steer young minds toward excellence. No. I was meant to teach because I love to laugh! A classroom is a laugh lab. I miss that. I absorbed valuable information from those long, unpaid, eighteen weeks of shadowing real teachers and my tours teaching eighth grade math and high school business communication.

By the way, student-teaching is a racket. Isn't it ironic that one of the lowest paid, yet most highly educated professional groups, inducts its own into the field with up to one work year minus income? Teachers also must purchase their own raises by earning higher degrees.

They do get legislated increases, but those raises rarely match inflation, talent, or effort. Once, the Tennessee teacher raise was only enough to buy one fifty-cent soft drink per day, so the teachers' union protested a Department of Education meeting by somehow parking multiple soft drink company semi-trucks in the Tennessee State Capitol Building parking lot.

Toward the end of my student teaching assignment, I surveyed my pupils for feedback on my teaching skills. I begged them to be honest. They were. Here are a few of their suggestions:

Give lots of praise.
Don't be a pushover.
Get to know <u>all</u> of your students, not just the obnoxious ones.
Don't talk the entire class. We are trying to concentrate.
Don't talk about the band so much. I don't like the band.
I don't care about the band.

Those were all good points, but I learned the most from Wilson. As I prepared for the principal's final observation in *The Giver's* ninth-grade typing class, I confessed to the students, "I hope nothing goes wrong during my evaluation. I will freak out if I mess up or the computers don't work!"

Wilson said, "You know Mrs. Dyer, he'll understand if something don't work. I mean, you know, *shift* happens."

Good sports Bug and Hot for Teacher.
Faculty basketball game.

Theory 3: Teachers are the most entertaining people on the planet.

They have to be. Reader, think back through all of your years in school. From kindergarten to high school to college, which teacher stands out in your memory? Who was your favorite? Picturing someone? Now, was that teacher an expert in Bloom's Taxonomy, Maslow's Hierarchy of Needs, or cross-curricular planning with informational text? Did you love him because he held three math degrees? Did you love her because she actually spoke fluent Latin? No. My guess is that your favorite teacher stands out for one primary reason: entertainment value.

Many folks are led to teaching because they *want* to entertain. They need a stage. The classroom is the perfect theater. The audience is required by law to attend. Real lives of faculty and staff are fodder for tragedy, romance, and comic relief.

Teachers bring the noise.

Some teachers get loud. Let's call them Yellers. Many Yellers are also Bellers. Bellers value noise as an instructional strategy. They blow whistles. They cadence clap students into submission. They drop text books on desktops to test whether a student is asleep or stoned.

Let's take it back a bit to the touron (defined: half tourist, half moron) infested school zones of Sevier County, Tennessee, the gateway to Great Smoky Mountains National Park. There, my dear family friend Tush taught next door to a Yeller/Beller. She told me, "[That teacher] would not stop ringing that dang bell. So, one day as I left school, I stole the bell. The next morning, I heard her let out a yell like no other, 'Where's my bell?' She blamed every child in her room for stealing the bell. On the last day of school, I snuck the bell behind a stack of books. When Yeller/Beller was cleaning up to go home for summer she laughed and said, "I didn't know I put that bell there!"

Teachers are pranksters.

They have to be. They say the same things over and over and must inject humor. My cousin Mooch is one of the funniest people I know. Mooch started the "Fake Rat Project" with a Halloween toy rat who bore flashing red eyes. Mooch hid the rat and declared a rule that whoever found the rat had to relocate it. Mooch and the Rat caused horror and hysterics, not to mention a few midday teacher costume changes. My typing course cohort Red Hot Backspace always started the school year with routes through Goodwill thrift shops. We procured cheap lamps, shelving, etc. For some reason, I urged Red Hot to go in on $20 worth of hideously tacky objects and put them all over the school. Red Hot asked me, "Why in the world do you want to do this?"

I explained, "So, when I see this random stuff in the library, teacher workroom, or a friend's classroom, I will have a reason to laugh." We set a pink goose ceramic soap dish on the faculty bathroom counter. The custodian even filled it with a bar of Dial! We tortured colleague Scone-Ad (home economics). We snuck a picture frame that actually had an '80s era prom photo of some random guy onto her desk. We added a Post-it note that read, "I still love you." She freaked out and called her husband. We never told the truth. Ah, I do miss teaching. Well, being a teacher. Well, being in a building with teachers.

Teachers get down.

Why do students always want to make teachers dance? And why is it that only the chubby teachers *will* actually dance? I jiggled through a flash mob, taught my eighth-grade math students a ruler-integer music routine, and broke it down at the prom. Schoolteacher dancing is tricky. You must show G-Rated proficiency; you can NOT be suggestive. Also, you should be with the times. You can't Twist or Shag if the children are Whipping and Nae Nae-ing. I saw way too many teachers do the Macarena. Maybe when teachers embarrass themselves on students' behalf, they earn student trust. Still, it appears teachers are frequently, and unfortunately, called to dance. They can't even slide by unnoticed. I was forced to chaperone a middle school dance. Luckily, because almost all the students were bus riders, the dance started at 3:45 p.m. The teacher who weren't chaperones had to exit without being seen, else they'd be dragged into the gym for another hour of torture. Sure enough, Ms. F choked under pressure. Or, perhaps her obese physique made her take the shortest route out. Regardless, students spotted her and yelled, "Ms. F, come dance with us!" She rolled her eyes, said okay, then walked directly onto the dance floor and joined the line dance. Ya'll, she flat out broke it down to the Cupid Shuffle. She knew every move and got it to the entire song without ever putting down her pocket book. If I had to guess, I'd say some old science teacher invented Fortnite.

Teachers make their own fun.

My high school biology teacher Bufe tortured ambitious honors students by offering an A+ on the entire fetal pig dissection project if we pulled the pig's brain and spinal cord out, completely intact. My neurotic, genius, now chemical engineer friend TRO broke out in a cold sweat mini-hacking that baby pig with tweezers and tiny scalpels. She was our valedictorian. Bufe also held weekly raffles to raise money for the soccer team. Since gambling was illegal in Tennessee then, he "sold" us Solo cups with numbers on the bottom. $1 per cup. He shuffled the cups like a magician. Winners won T-shirts and game tickets.

Teachers demonstrate romance.

In Columbus, Georgia, Delicious worked with a pervy assistant principal who, literally, locked her in his office and chased her around a desk, begging for "just one little kiss." He did stop to squirt breath spray into his mouth. It was the mid 70's. The King of Kodak, my high school geography teacher, was also the king of romance! Every Friday, he hosted a dating game. He cut a small heart into a piece of notebook paper. He laid the paper on the overhead projector and shut off the lights. He chose a female student to come up front and stand in the overhead-projected heart spotlight. The girl chose a number that correlated to another student in the King's roll book. The boy met the girl in the light. Then, the King spun his globe to determine where they would go on their fictional date. Once, my lovely friend Mare got set up with my cousin Roscoe. They were destined for love in Nicaragua! I think she was excited, but she never admitted it. The romance category is one place where educated should NOT use the "I do. We do. You do" method of instruction.

Public school teachers make amusing public mistakes.

Teachers are tired. Teachers get punchy. Teachers are over-stimulated throughout the day. So, teachers mess up. Sometimes by accident. Sometimes on purpose. Delicious is not a housekeeper.

Laundry piled up at our house, and every morning was harried. Well, one good old day at G-P, Delicious was strolling the rows, speaking in blank verse, forcing *Hamlet* onto teenagers, while a gaggle of girls giggled. For half an hour. Finally, she confronted them and asked, "Okay, y'all are being rude while I teach. What is the deal?"

One said, "We're sorry Mrs. Delicious, but you've got panty hose coming out of your britches." I'm not sure how she did this, but Delicious had put on her polyester Kmart (I'm sure) black pants and a pair of nude hose were stuck inside, leg for leg. Basically, she looked like the house in the *The Wizard of Oz* with the Wicked Witch's socks uncurled and exposed. She had dragged those empty tan feet around all morning. I wondered how she got dressed without noticing her ghost twin legs, but then I remembered how she threw her back out putting on jazzercize tights back in '86.

To the delight of night school Comp 101 students at a local junior college, Delicious dragged her tired body to class and slung her tote bag hard to the top of her desk in front of the class. When that cotton bag struck the Formica, Delicious's Preparation H fell out. She told me, "That Preparation H tube shot across the floor like a torpedo! I had to search under all the desks to retrieve it!"

My old principal, Mr. Z, was tough and tall and bragged to students that he could do a mid-air karate kick. Well, he did. But, at the height of his exhibition, he split his pants. Wide open.

I taught at a "rough," rowdy middle school my first year of teaching. My daily classroom motto (which I muttered all day long to myself) was "Don't cuss, don't cry, don't quit." I made it all the way to May — but I still showed my tail. Worn out by my sometimes-rude students, many of whom I still stay in contact with, I lost my cool. I was holding a stack of math workbooks and thought, *I am so freakin' mad I'm going to throw these across the room!* I did it. I hurled 30 books across the room and watched them smack then slide down the cinderblock wall, stunning students. Then I put on a You-Tube worthy twenty-minute tirade. It was quite a show. The students loved it! I learned a lesson from those workbooks: throwing them was more effective than assigning them. The students paid attention for a whole ten minutes after my tantrum.

Teachers solve problems with flare.

My sweet, typically soft-spoken, algebra teacher Right Angle, frustrated with our lack of understanding, shocked us one day. He jumped from his chair and leapt across his desk and out the door. He re-entered and sat down. Then, he dived under his desk and crawled out the door. He re-entered and sat down. Finally, he stood and sauntered out the door. When he returned, a student asked, "Right Angle, are you okay?"

He answered with his pointer finger in the air and his voice in a lilt, "I'm just demonstrating that there's more than *one* way to solve a problem!" It was a miracle he didn't throw out his back. Teachers do that a lot, too.

Teachers sneak like Pink Panther.

Teachers are trapped during the workday. They can't leave campus. Delicious was notorious for sending students on off-campus errands (this was way before teacher evaluations and Common Core Standards). Think of the movie *Dazed and Confused*. Delicious gave a senior boy her car keys and had him take her car, which she called Greenie, to the car wash on Highway 321. She also sent students to Proffitt's Deli to bring back her lunch. Of course, they were compensated with temporary freedom and chili dogs. She continued the tradition until a boy brought back a bunch of Budweiser cans and announced to Delicious, "Look what we found in your trunk!"

Speaking of changing times, Delicious never quite adjusted to the age of technology. In the late '90s her school got a set of teacher computers and Delicious got her first email account. The trainer explained, "Decide on a password and tell no one what it is." Well, Delicious sat through the long meeting, straining to guard her new key to warp-speed, limitless communication. But, she finally broke, telling her best friend, "I can't take this anymore! I don't like keeping secrets. I am telling you my password."

The much younger, tech savvy teacher Glassy Eyes sighed, "Okay, what is it?"

Delicious whispered through her clenched jaw, "*Computer.*"

Teachers demonstrate irony.

To students, teachers are wonderful listeners. To in-service trainers, teachers are *terrible* listeners. Teachers love to talk. And since they are accustomed to dynamic, harried days, teachers don't sit still very well. They all end up with ADHD. Who wants to explain stuff all day and then listen to someone else explain stuff? It's tough. It's like listening to yourself explain stuff. Geez. I got so tired of my own voice!

An education buddy once told me that teachers are, ironically, notorious for modeling the specific behaviors they personally hate in students. For example, teachers who want their classrooms super quiet are the chattiest in meetings. The ones who value punctuality are late to training. He quipped, "If you spot it, you've got it!"

Teacher diets are comics.

Usually, in-service trainers schmooze the audience with door prizes, school supplies, breaks, and food. Teachers love food. Just like students. What is that all about? They'll eat anything at any time on any day. I had pizza and cake before 9 a.m. numerous school days. After I enjoyed three desserts during one late summer in-service, a table-mate teacher friend said to me, as she gobbled down her own sweet buffet, "I can't start my diet until I have students."

Sweater Vest Romeo is dressed to test.

Theory 4: The only thing worse than teacher fashion is *substitute* teacher fashion.

A few years ago, along with the rest of middle class America, I was affected by the recession. Forced to leave the daily domestic bliss of housewifery behind, I opted to avoid returning to my old career—retail banking. Instead, in stubborn denial, I chose a much lower paid profession. I chose to test the waters of public education. I signed up to be a substitute teacher. Little did I know that I'd eventually get certified and become a full-time educator.

In Theory 3, I explained the ways in which teachers engage their audiences. One crucial element in school performance is wardrobe.

Fashion in schools is an often-controversial issue, but typically the combatants are students and administrators. For example, at Powell High, the principal spot checked the student body's bodies all at once. He played the Top 40 song that goes "Shake it like a Polaroid picture" over the intercom system and announced, "Teachers, look around your classrooms. If you see any butts, bellies, or boobs, send 'em to the office!"

Well, what about teacher fashion? What about professionalism? What about "looking authoritative" while also being able to crawl under tables and, well, chase people? Teachers try. They really do. But keep in mind that teaching is not a lucrative career. And, subs, per day, gross around half what first year teachers do, which ain't much.

So, back at the bottom of the recession, I rode an elevator to the top of the Knox County Schools Central Office Building to sit through a long day of substitute teacher training. The old building's original construction crew must have run out of bricks. When I stepped off the elevator into a dusty, narrow hallway, I felt like Gulliver, for two reasons. First, the oppressive ceiling was a squatty seven feet high. Second, the Lilliputian trainer looked as though he'd been measured then assigned to work in the short space.

During the grueling day-long course, the Lollipop Kid explained that subs grossed $67 a day and that, after taxes, I'd net about $50. Plus, paychecks fell on the 25th of the month *following* the month of the day you subbed. For example: Work August 1-3 and gross $201. Net $150 on September 25. Really? I felt my soul leave my body and hover over the Target-shirted, Cato's-capris'd, Yellow-Box sandaled crowd. The tiny man then explained how we needed to dress professionally. He warned that we might have to rush out the door to a job so he advised we lay out our clothes the night before. Then he forced us to watch a gruesome video on bloodborne pathogens. I assume — and hope I don't offend anyone by saying this — that many subs come to the job because they need money. I certainly did. I spent $72 on a drug test, background check, and fingerprints. Before I could hand out worksheets and do a playground headcount, Knox County had to know, for sure, that I wasn't a meth-addicted child molester.

I heard "professional" but I saw "bloodborne pathogens." I heard "academic" but I saw a PowerPoint about "hormones." I heard "look serious" and I saw instructions on handling student fist-fights.

I envisioned my future substitute teacher outfit folded on a chair in my bedroom. I balanced the demands of administrators and the needs of my blood and saliva-spewing hormonal students and settled on a substitute wardrobe motto: "Keep it cheap and keep *them* covered."

I called Delicious to gripe. She laughed and advised, "First of all, don't worry about tucking anything in. I haven't tucked a shirt in or worn a belt since the '70s. Just go to Walmart and get two pairs of black britches. Make *sure* you wear comfortable shoes. Bug, just think about what your old teachers and subs used to wear!"

Let's take a walk down school memory lane and recall our favorite teacher duds from days gone by, shall we?

Coaching shorts made me nervous. There was plenty of polyester around back then. Why couldn't manufacturers give those men two or three more inches? I lived in fear of my beloved teachers striking The Thinker pose and scarring me for life.

If you work with someone who still pulls on a denim jumper, call TLC's show, *What Not to Wear*. Please. Why would anyone lay that much denim across her body? It's heavy, hot, and flattens all the wrong parts. And, no matter how hard you try, you'll never find the right shoes to go with a jumper.

Some outfits are so "strong" they've survived decades. From chalkboards to laptops, from good old recess to lunchroom overregulation, from holding students accountable for their behavior to now over diagnosing and blaming teachers for, well, everything, one constant has remained: The sweater that tells a story. Common Core standards mandate that teachers use informational text in the classroom. Graphic novels stitched onto wool do not count. If you see Facebook and Instagram posts of "tacky sweater parties" and your outfit from Monday is someone's social media cover photo, you may want to put some new blouses on layaway.

Speaking of grossness, once you wear an outfit to school, it is tarnished. Think Seinfeld's "book in the bathroom" episode. Tall Child told me, "One good thing about teaching is that you can wear your regular clothes to work, and not have two wardrobes." Wrong, again, Tall Child. Teachers and subs contact and contract dust, ink, paint, chalk, toner, throw-up, viruses, bloodborne pathogens, etc. From personal experience, I can assure you that, indeed, cooties are real. Also, food on the fly is messy. Try eating lunch from bell to bell, while praying a student doesn't interrupt your break. My colleague Red Hot used to turn off the lights and lock the door. We dined by floating screensaver light.

When I subbed and taught junior high, I embraced the experience full force. I bought long-sleeved T-shirts from a large retailer. I wore cheap black britches that were short in the stride and hem length. A female teenage student once looked me over and said, "Mrs. Bug, you be floodin', huh?"

Lucky for me, we had a tornado drill that day. As wind and rain assaulted the roof, I paced the hallway to make sure students sat in safe position. I spotted the girl and said, "Good thing I wore these pants, huh?"

My neighbor once scolded me for not recycling. Well, I'll have the community know that my teacher work blouses eventually became pajamas. Those pajamas became painting and yard work shirts. Those thinned yard work shirts became dust rags. That's a solid deal for a seven-dollar shirt and very kind to the environment. My cousin Moon said he wanted disposable furniture. I found the next best thing, disposable clothing. By the way, I want the media, signage, and people in general to stop telling me to "save the planet." That is a daunting task. Movies are made about it. When students said something to that effect, I said, "Can't. I don't have a cape." I totally would have worn a cape, but never a story sweater. You're welcome, boys and girls.

My wardrobe evolved as I observed my fellow educators. *The Giver* "supported" every club in school by buying its fundraising T-shirts. Who can admonish a teacher who is rooting for the track team and raising money for the drama club while fighting cancer, Alzheimer's, and bullies every week? She accessorized with a bedazzled lanyard and I.D. badge.

My science teacher buddy, whom I nicknamed Sugar Bear because he loves Dr. Pepper and because he's so stinking cute, wears his Sunday church clothes to school every Monday. He just lays the whole outfit in a chair after worship services. His motto? "God first. Laundry second."

Another co-worker confessed that she buys no-iron clothes because sometimes she puts her work clothes on before she goes to bed so she can sleep an extra fifteen minutes. Teachers are tired.

White sandals. Just don't. Forget about the calendar. White sandals are always wrong. So are unpainted toenails. Gross.

Cardigans with a modest sleeveless top are a must. Students in? Sweater on. Students out? Sweater off. Layers combat hot flashes, cold meeting rooms, and exposure to the elements via fire drills. Most importantly, an extra layer keeps you from over-revealing middle-aged body parts. I taught in a computer lab. I can't tell you how many times teenage boys asked Red Hot and me to take over their mice and show them how to navigate Excel spreadsheets.

Years later, I returned to my original yuck-job, banking, I had to buy all new work clothes. And high heels. I missed my comfortable, disposable teacher drag. No thought and little effort was required. Then. I mean, I didn't wear the *same* pants every day – I just wore the same *pants* every day.

Here's my old school wardrobe:
2 pairs black slacks
2 pairs gray slacks
1 pair dark jeans for blue jean Fridays– NOT tight, at least not tight on purpose.
5 solid sleeveless tops
5 solid cardigans
School T-shirt. Go team!
Brown flats
Black Sketchers
Crocs. Yes. Sorry. I still have them. They're animal print. That counts for something, right? Animal print is always in style.

I tried to liven up my look with earrings, but by the first round of standardized testing, bling was too much work. I usually wore one of two pairs: $2.88 gold and silver hoops. My ten-dollar watch was gold *and* silver so I wore it every day.

I miss teenagers. I loved to stop class, take random polls, and record student responses so I could either post them on Facebook or share them with Delicious for laughs. One day, I quizzed my freshmen, "What advice would you give teachers and subs on how to dress?" My high school freshmen responded:

> *Don't shop at an old person store.*
> *Don't wear too much foundation and then no mascara.*
> *Yes, please wear lipstick!*
> *Look professional. Wear skirts.*
> *Skirts don't go with nurse shoes.*
> *Socks and sandals make me sick.*
> *Don't mix patterns.*
> *Too many clashing colors look bad.*
> *One teacher dressed like Princess Diana. Long dresses, short hair.*
> *Don't wear old lady perfume.*
> *Don't dress like students.*

I interrupted, "What about the male teachers?" I heard:

> *I hate when the men teachers are all baggy.*
> *Tuck your shirt in and look proper!*
> *Wear khakis.*
> *And Polos.*
> *Don't wear tennis shoes. Wear dress shoes.*
> *We don't want to see chest hair. I mean, we can't* see *it, but we can see the little dots under the shirt.*

I remarked, "Wow. Y'all really have high expectations!"

One student consoled, "Well, you *should* take a lazy day *sometimes*. Wear tennis shoes on Fridays."

Sharky makes frenemies on Gravy and BBJ's farm.

Theory 5: You should be nice to everyone you meet because you *will* meet again, *especially* if you weren't nice in the first place.

Let me finally explain why we call my mother Delicious. My cousin, whom we call Roscoe for his obsession with *The Dukes of Hazard*, played basketball for Virginia Tech. The players decided to give each member of the mama fan gaggle a nickname. Roscoe's mama carried a noticeable donk, so they deemed her "Big Booty J" or "BBJ" for short. My mama went to lots of games with her, so the boys knew her well. Mama's colorful blouses stretch across her well-endowed bosom. Her chandelier earrings swish below her short, black, curly hair. She always carries a drink, typically diet blueberry juice, somehow filled *above* the rim of a twenty-ounce

Styrofoam cup that threatens pocketbooks in bleachers across the South. And she loves to toss back popcorn and peanuts between lipsticked smiles and affirmations. Appropriately, the boys named her "Delicious D." Who says athletes don't appreciate grammar and mechanics? Alliteration is alive and well in college basketball.

While Delicious is eccentric, she's also a great teacher. Delicious beat maxims into my brain, especially during four years of driving to and from high school together. She taught at my school, or should I say, I attended hers. I had the typically limited social life of any only child from a holler, so we were pretty much together 24 hours a day. I mean, I couldn't skip school because she would notice I wasn't in the passenger seat. Maybe. She did drive 30 miles down Interstate 40 West with huge pruning shears on the hood. I wonder how many fellow drivers thought, "Why is that woman blaring Three Dog Night's 'One is the loneliest number' with pruning shears on the hood of her car?"

Anyway, during our 45-minute commute from Catlettsburg to Gatlinburg, which took us through a one-way section called The Spur in Great Smoky Mountains National Park, I listened and learned. One of Mama's favorite lessons is "Be nice to everyone you meet." My Grandmama, mother to Delicious and known here as "Buddy," used to say it another way: "It doesn't cost a dime to be a gentleman."

This Theory has played out over and over in my life, but I'm going to illustrate with two examples. In the first, Delicious is the instigator. In the second, I am the victim, until I am the victor!

Example 1: Delicious was shopping at The Kmart (in The South, store names are amped up with the article "The," as in The Walmart, The Exxon, The Co-Op). Perhaps she was balancing a Styrofoam cup of Coca-Cola or pouring a plastic sleeve of peanuts through her Revlon Wine with Everything lips. Perhaps she wasn't paying attention, but Delicious made a driving error in the parking lot of The Kmart. A female driver behind her angrily honked, and Delicious flipped her The Bird. As the woman—likely aghast at the obscene gesture—cruised by, Delicious peered into the driver's window to give the lady the stink eye and spotted her co-worker and friend of twenty years! What did Delicious do? She "laid low," flipped the visor down, and peeled out of the parking lot in a flash of embarrassment. She never apologized. She never admitted her sin. She simply hoped her co-worker never noticed her in the first place. But, she's endured the guilty memory and the nagging curiosity for decades. Delicious learned her lesson and has not flipped The Bird *in The Kmart* parking lot since. Why The Kmart, not The Walmart, you ask? The Kmart had layaway.

Example 2: Picture me, Bug, twenty pounds lighter (yay) twenty years ago, all decked out in a navy-blue business suit, panty hose, and taupe high heels. Painful, neutral, nervous shoes: taupe. The suit jacket did its best to conceal the professional woman's enemy: giant boobs. I prayed the minimizer bra kept its promise. Taupe means business. Boobs mean bimbo. I was one month away from graduating from The University of Tennessee and was as broke as a haint. (A haint is a low-class ghost who basically hangs around and harasses. Use it in a sentence? Sure: Haints haint.)

Full of self-confidence with a touch of naiveté, I typed up a resume` and cover letter in UT's Career Services Center and set out to bust the world wide open, professionally speaking, beginning with downtown Knoxville, Tennessee. Reader, you remember attempting the jump from school to career. You remember nervously checking your lipstick and dissolving an Altoid in the elevator. It's a scary time, isn't it?

My first stop was Home [Local] Bank, simply because I was familiar with it. Delicious banks there, and my old babysitter worked the drive-through in Sevierville. I planned to drop off my documents, give my practiced not-too-feminine, not-too-masculine handshake, and politely introduce myself to the director of human resources, who would no-doubt be impressed by my finance degree, outgoing personality, confident handshake, and taupe shoes. The receptionist said, "Thank you for your resume, but Mr. Mumble doesn't usually talk to anyone unless he calls you for an interview."

I replied, "Well, I am about to graduate and just need one second of his time to introduce myself." (I was coached at the UT Career Center to personally hand off my resume, make eye contact, use the handshake, etc., to increase my chances of a call back.) No deal at Home [Local] Bank. But, Mr. Mumble did, just at *that* second, open his office door and walk right into the room! I pounced, "Good morning, Mr. Mumble. May I speak with you for just a moment?" Mr. Mumble grumbled, avoided eye contact, and walked off. For a human resources director, he didn't act human at all! Needless to say, I ended up working for another bank. About five years into my career I was promoted to be branch manager of its main office (whoop whoop!). The first day on the job, I met my staff, which included a lady with the common surname Mumble. We got to know one another, and I found out that she was married to THE Mr. Mumble at Home [Local] Bank. What?!? I was nice to Mrs. Mumble, though I admit I cut her zero slack. I felt sorry for her; after all, she was married to the sub-human human resources officer, but, boy did I get a chuckle out of being her boss. Poetic justice?

By the way, Mr. Mumble studies handwriting psychology. Mrs. Mumble, who never knew about the embarrassing rejection back in '95, took one of my notes home for him to analyze. He said I was "open and friendly, but in a hurry." I'd like to analyze his handwriting. I could humble Mr. Mumble if I told him that every time Mrs. Mumble brought her dish "Cherry Yum-Yum" to work to share, we all dipped out kind paper bowls full, bragged on the flavor, and dumped the Cool-whip compote concoction into the shred bin because we'd each witnessed her skip hand-washing in the ladies' room. Must every business post a bathroom sign that reads, "Employees must wash their hands?" Really? Evolve! I'd also like to tell Mr. Mumble he may be good at reading handwriting, but he misread 22-year-old me. I hate being misunderstood, don't you? He should have been nice to me in the first place.

Balloon Girl admonishes Sharky and Buzz.

Theory 6: Don't judge a woman by her accent or her breast size.

Throughout my life, I've endured harassment and teasing about two prominent personal characteristics: my accent and my breast size. I am not complaining, just explaining. Delicious taught me to never remark about someone's appearance. It is cruel to negatively comment on unchangeable physical characteristics of fellow human beings.

Winston Churchill once stated, "There is no more beautiful sound than the voice of an educated Southern woman." The women of my mother's family come from the Deep South—Georgia and Alabama. Southern drawls drape their phrases like Spanish moss softens live oak branches. I'd like to say I sound like Dixie Carter in "Designing Women," but I sound more like Tennessee's queen of basketball and daughter of tobacco, the late great Pat Summitt. If a Deep Southern woman's accent is coconut rum, mine is sour mash. I am an East Tennessean. We have our own sound. My words clang and clash like the breaking down of a moonshine still. I don't sound beautiful, Mr. Churchill. I actually sound, well, in accent and dialect anyway, dumb. Thankfully, Delicious beat grammar and mechanics into my brain on that Smoky Mountain school commute, so, if you listen closely, you realize I am Harbrace Handbook proficient.

One summer in high school, I attended Tennessee Governor's School for the Humanities in Martin, Tennessee, in the northwest corner of the state. Basically, it's language arts nerd camp. Shakespeare + a classroom in July = not cool. The high-brow crowd had a heyday with my dialect. As Kenny Chesney would croon, "Back where I come from" (Gatlinburg), we all sounded about the same, but when I got to Governor's School, I was called out, mercilessly. That was tough on my fifteen-year-old soul, which was already showing up at nerd camp with size 34DD boobies and praying I wouldn't have to swim. My roommate's finding my mother's letter to me, which detailed how Delicious had dipped our beagles for fleas, was no help. I tried to soften my twang, employ the other campers' catch-phrases, and convince them I had a brain, but ended up sounding ridiculous, especially when I returned to the hollers. I should have left the fake voice in Martin, like Michigan-born Madonna should leave her British accent in London. Regardless, I was in a weird little campus heaven with that crowd. It was a verbal free-fire zone and I could say whatever I wanted and KNOW I was understood (and tolerated). Yes, we were innocent and geeky, but witty people are often edgy in language and not in deed. Our biggest risks were taking food from the cafeteria and staying up past curfew. But, we let each other have it. One guy bragged that he was the stud of his debate team. His name was Kevin. So, some genius tagged him and we all called him Kevin the Master Debater for a month. Let's hope that didn't follow him home to Memphis. Each morning, a counselor posted a word of the day, followed by its definition and samples of its usage in sentences, on the dorm building door. One morning, some student replaced the flyer with one that read, "Today's word is legs. Spread the word."

In college, my East Tennessee accent drew harassment from romantic competition. I was on a date with a really cute frat boy when his "sorority sister" questioned me in a valley-girl condescending tone, "Oh my goodness, your accent is so thick. I've never heard anything like it! Where are you from?"

I replied (typed phonetically here), "Well, I'm French. I grew up in Pea jhion four czhay, which is just east of Ville` day Seveeyay." (Pigeon Forge, just east of Sevierville.) Frat boy laughed. Sorority sister didn't.

An author friend suggested I post video trailers for my books to YouTube. Another writer told me it's the second largest search engine behind Google. I know a guy who can film me, and I know the marketing is worthwhile, but I am extremely self-conscious about how my voice sounds through a microphone. Think Ellie Mae; just subtract the bailing twine belt and add pollen-induced hoarseness, or, as we say in the hollers, a frog in my throat. Ugh. I fear that my uneducated-*sounding* self would turn off potential readers.

Red Hot Backspace, also sports a country accent and a nice set of knockers. We often worried aloud, and truly believed, that because of these combos, our northern-born colleagues underestimated our academic and professional abilities. Frustrated, they smirked and waded their way through our swamp of colloquialisms, but they eventually cottoned up to us. Well, most of them.

In addition to my twang, my breasts have always been points of intrigue to many. My breasts have driven me crazy most of my life. Don't get me wrong. I appreciate being well-endowed. A lot of confidence comes with breast size. Maybe watching Miss Piggy swat other Muppets down with her boobs helped me. I felt empowered by her feminine yet confident example. I had something most girls wanted and couldn't have, until silicone came along. At least I could still brag, "Mine are real." But I'm not sure that's a good thing, especially at my age and size. At least the fake ones are perky. If mine were a yoga position, they'd be Downward Dogs.

As far as the "girls" go, I did my best to conceal them as I taught high school freshmen. I always wore tight camisoles, which Red Hot's daughter Suspenders calls "squeezers," over my high-dollar, rib-torturing bras. Just after Tall Child and I married, I told him that although I came with little money, he should consider my boobs as a dowry since many of his friends had to purchase their wives' attributes.

In college, because of the boobs, boys mistook me for a wild girl. In the early '90s, at The University of Tennessee, fashion trends called for tight tops. On a teacher's child strict budget, I struggled to be in style and had limited clothing choices, so my girls were on display. I got lots of attention from boys, but their expectations were as large as what they *wanted* to see. And, I was a good girl. So, they often called me a tease, based only on what I looked like! At least they had goals.

In high school no one called me a tease because Delicious was there to make sure all the boys knew I would remain a virgin. But, she couldn't protect me when I ran track. Trying to keep my royal blue Umbro shorts from sliding up my rear to expose my lily-white thighs was bad enough, but that was before sports bras. I was all over the place as I pounded around the track, "running" the 880. My most memorable moment came as my team, the Gatlinburg-Pittman Highlanders, raced against the Seymour Eagles. I had a bad crush on a Seymour boy, and he was on their track team. I remember plodding slowly down the long side of the track, opposite where he sat with his teammates, and hearing a chant of some sort. As I rounded the turn, the chant became louder and clearer. Amid Reeboks hitting pavement and labored breaths, I heard, "Boom chugga lugga lugga. Boom chugga lugga lugga. Boom chugga lugga lugga." Then it dawned on me. They were chanting with the rhythm of my bouncing breasts! I closed my elbows in toward my chest to try to control things, but it was hopeless. I gave up and let it all hang out, even my thighs. I crossed the finish line in last place, caught my breath, then climbed straight up the bleachers to confront the crowd of skinny teenage goober boys. I said, "I'm glad y'all enjoyed the race. If you liked that, you should see me dance!" Oh, they liked it, alright. That boy took me to the prom. Boobyah!

'80s Bug. Like. The. Wind.

Theory 7: Play a sport. Even if you suck at it.

Do any of you tape important info inside your kitchen cabinets? Say you are searching for Cheez-Its. If you open one of my cabinet doors, you'll spot wine labels, a love note from Tall Child, phone numbers to my favorite restaurants, and, thanks to Delicious's old 35mm camera, a perfectly captured specimen of supreme athleticism: me, at age nine, hurdling a broomstick balanced between two lawn chairs in my grandmama's back yard. The hurdling photo is crucial: it proves that I can be athletic.

Or least that I once was.

Well, in that moment anyway.

I asked Tall Child, who was a standout Bearden High School and Hiwassee College basketball player, "Did you ever play a sport and fail?"

He answered, "No. Why, are you going to write about me?"

I said, "Well, I'm writing about NOT being good."

He emphasized, "Not being good in sports is something I know nothing about."

True. Tall Child is a natural athlete. He has a fierce tennis serve, a quick bat, a smooth golf swing, and a flawless jump shot, even in his fifties. Heck, I have seen him trip only one time. He was playing softball, and as he walked through the grass to take his centerfield spot, he stumbled. He turned angrily and stared down a specific spot on the ground, as if to say, "Who do you think you are, tripping *me*, you amateur dirt clod?"

I am the oldest of ten first cousins, most of whom are above-average, if not collegiate-level athletes. Our grandfather played baseball, golf, and basketball for The University of Georgia. His two sons played basketball for Auburn and The University of Tennessee at Chattanooga. Cousin Roscoe played basketball at Virginia Tech. Cousin A-Boo conquered Vanderbilt University with a golf scholarship. PGA dynamo Brandt Snedeker is one of her closest friends. She introduced him to his wife. I asked her back then, "Why didn't you try to date Brandt? He's cute and sweet."

She explained, "Bug, I'm built like a female golfer, not a pro golfer's wife." I suppose if Tall Child were a professional golfer, I'd have to be his caddy, just because of the forgiving outfit. I could never run out to hug someone on national TV.

So, sports and competitiveness are part of our family culture. We all played. It was expected. My Grandmama once remarked, "If you drive through Sevier County with your window rolled down, somebody will throw a trophy in your car!"

Yep. My whole family played. And I sucked.

When my cousins and I were little, the "grown-ups" would set up competitions—for their entertainment. There are ten of us, all born in one decade. I'm the oldest, and Property Brother (nicknamed for his artful restoration skills) is the youngest. Big Booty J, an elementary school teacher, announced the rules and instructions with demonstrative flair, as in, "Alright, every single one of you WILL compete." Not only did the grown-ups demand participation, but they also coached from the sidelines. Many of them were coaches, anyway. Our games included one-on-one basketball tournaments, horse, hurdles, hula-hooping, the long jump, the standing broad jump, and foot races. Well, I stunk it up in everything physical. I also kicked myself in the rear-end as I ran, on purpose, as a self-esteem-defense tactic. Instead of talking about how I was twenty yards behind my cousins, the grown-ups talked about how I kicked my behind when I ran.

In bad weather we had spelling bees, coloring contests, and dance competitions. Grandmama Buddy liked to say and demonstrate, "Shake your head, not just your body." Delicious requested my "dirty dawg" move. Imagine a pasty white freckled nine-year-old with a Little Debbie chubby tummy hula-hooping, minus the hoop. I'm not a good dancer, but I watched "Soul Train" back then. I picked up the hip-swiveling dirty dawg move, and at least gained applause, if not a recycled trophy from some family member's glory days. And, we ALL clogged. Actually, my first memory of dancing took place in Buddy's Columbus, Georgia, bedroom. She played the Osborne Brothers' recording of Felice and Boudleaux Bryant's "Rocky Top" from a 45 on her record player. We clogged and tried to croon "Tennessee, ee, ee, ee..." and see which grandchild held the last "ee" the longest.

Always competing.

The best dancer was, and still is, Roscoe. A few years ago, Roscoe owned one of those old timey photo booths in New Orleans. Katrina washed him out of business, but he kept the costumes. The following Thanksgiving, he surprised us all with a dance tribute to honor Native Americans. He sported one colorful chief's headdress and one tiny loincloth. That's all. Roscoe is six-feet-seven, so the head feathers tickled the ceiling. Roscoe used a baseball bat to row his imaginary canoe to the beat of "Kung Fu Fighting" through the den. He amazed and stunned the crowd. Sharky, seven and obsessed with Davy Crockett at the time, happened to have a toy rifle with him. Between Roscoe's bump-grind-row routine, I heard Sharky "Pew, pew! Pew! Pew, pew!" He hid behind the furniture and did his best to kill the Comanche. Uncle Trout hid, too, fearing a lap-dance.

Unfortunately, the forced athleticism didn't end in our living room dance contests and dandelion-riddled yards. Delicious signed me up to be a cheerleader in kindergarten. I, with my fair-skinned, often red-headed Appalachian classmates of Pigeon Forge Elementary School, who didn't look too good in orange and black polyester, loved to chant these two ditties to rally the grasscutters' football team:

Grandmama Moses, sick in bed,
She's got the ring-a-ding fever, and this is what she said:
Take two steps back and turn around,
Do the shimmy shimmy shake and touch the ground.
Big daddy, little daddy, Susie Q
C'mon boys, we're rootin' for you.

Another favorite:

Boys got the muscles, teachers got the brains,
Girls got the sexy legs so we win the game!
Go Tigers!

Political correctness forbids such cheers these days. God forbid women have sexy legs and men have muscles. I didn't mind cheerleading too much. Our teacher was sweet, the concession stand was close by, and it was really neat to rub the pompon plastic between my hands and quadruple the size of my shaker. I respect cheerleaders as athletes, but I don't belong with them. I hate bows. They look like anchors. Maybe I watched too much Popeye. I also don't like to point my toes. It's too much work.

Delicious signed me up to take gymnastics, too. My question was this: What is the point of ever doing a head or handstand? If you fall, you hit your head. That can't be good. It could be painful. Also, what is the point of a cartwheel? To cover more ground? Maybe. Once, at Dollywood, a cousin said, "Let's hold hands and skip all the way to the Flooded Mine Ride so we'll get there faster." I swear it worked. He's an engineer now. By the way, I never mastered the headstand, which ultimately affected my keg stands in college.

Delicious signed me up for basketball in fifth grade. I had to change clothes in front of other girls, and I was already sprouting the space heaters. I hated sweating and got really annoyed when another girl bumped into me on the basketball court. Once, the coach had me throw the ball inbounds. This was a big moment for me: a moment of responsibility and leadership. I threw the ball toward my Pigeon Forge Tiger teammate, and an opposing player batted it back to me — three times in a row. That year (my only season), I scored one free throw and one regular shot. All-time career high: three points (game and season). Does that mean my average was three-tenths of a point per game if we had ten games? Yay, fractions! There were some good moments. Before practices, we walked down the hill to Shoney's, pooled our leftover lunch money, and shared hot fudge cakes.

Delicious signed me up for the Sevierville Sting Rays swim team in middle school. I continued swimming a couple of years in high school. I also sucked at swimming. Again, my boobs were an issue. Too much drag. I learned the importance of aerodynamics. Reasonably, I was not first pick for the relay teams. Big Booty J and Buddy came to cheer me on. Proud to display my slow, yet skillful swimming, I perched on the diving block, tightened my goggles, and took my mark. Then I dived in! Then I heard the pistol!

Disqualified.

Underwater, I realized the order is 1. Gun, 2. Jump. I jumped the swim gun. They had waited all day in the steaming humidity, and I got disqualified. Needless to say, I didn't draw much of a crowd after that non-performance. I can tell you this: an athletic family hates a choker. If you mess up on anything, you are a choker. For example, if you drop the mail, lean over to pick something up off the floor with the two-finger grasp (which often takes several attempts, doesn't it?) and miss, or burn supper, you hear, "Way to choke."

No experience is safe. After realizing that I was hopelessly infertile, Tall Child lamented on my behalf, "All that time you were a good girl in college because you were afraid of getting pregnant, you could have been wearing it out. Way to choke."

I replied, "True, but there's also dignity and personal self-worth."

Tall Child said, "Let's just say I had more fun at The University of Tennessee than you did."

Swim team *can* be fun when you have a tent, buddies, a cooler full of Cokes and Little Debbie Swiss Cake Rolls and know how to play Spades and Slap Jack. My love of tailgating was born beside the Sevierville City Pool.

My freshman year of high school, Delicious signed me up for track. Just like I sucked in in the 50-meter pool, I sucked on the 440-meter track. (Well, except for my entertaining, chant-provoking bouncers.) Delicious made me do it. She said that my being on some kind of team would look good on my college transcripts. My team practiced by running the arts and crafts loop down Glades and Buckhorn Roads in Gatlinburg. My best friends and I paced through the rhododendron-lined asphalt path banked by Smoky Mountain potters and painters. My coach, also my geography teacher, also known as the King of Kodak, Tennessee, was amazed at my body's aversion to speed. We solved the mystery. Back in the late eighties, a company called Whittle Communications broadcasted news programs called Channel One throughout public schools. Which, to be honest, felt a little socialist, which was quite threatening to the conservative "GDI" (God [Danged] Independent) crowd occupying the steep, wooded hills of East Tennessee. We barely had subdivisions, and our busiest community organizations were churches and sports teams. Anyway, one morning the teen science reporter on Channel One explained a medical condition in which some people's muscles don't ignite and get going the way others' do. The condition is called "slow-twitch muscle fibers." Finally, the King of Kodak knew why I was so sluggish. He nicknamed me "Slo-Jo," playing off his medical diagnosis and the then-famous Olympian Flo-Jo.

In individual races, I never, NEVER, beat anyone. In track or in swimming. That's right: I came in last place in every individual race I ever swam or ran. But, I loved the settings. I loved riding the bus to meets. I loved laughing with my friends and flirting with other girls' crushes. Most of all, I loved what swimming and running did for my appearance.

You know, when you grow up in an athletic family, are married to a former college basketball player, and are raising two sporty boys, you just can't let go of the dream of somehow being athletic. A few years ago, I stepped out of my Appalachian comfort zone. I signed up to play tennis. The tennis skirt is an interesting get-up. What does it say to you? The skirt said to me, "You'd better slim up, Hoss, because I've got two layers and big pockets for balls, right at your widest points." Nothing motivates one to exercise and eat well like a toned, tanned group of ladies with Levolor blind eyelids checking you out as your parts and you bounce around a tennis court. I was self-conscious. I told Tall Child, "I think I could be a decent tennis player if I had a good racquet."

He responded, "Bug, your level of athleticism is not worthy of that level of investment." I conceded and wrapped up my tennis season and career with a Walmart racquet.

I think I'm the same shape I was in high school (not *in* shape, just shape), but at least twenty pounds heavier. Math! Similar triangles, right? The ratio is the same, yet the shape is larger. I probably should do something about my hypotenuse. I suppose I could slow-twitch trot my way around my neighborhood at night and pray Gnome doesn't wander into the street while I'm exercising. Nah, I'd rather down Pinot Grigio and watch zombie shows with Tall Child. The three—wine, zombies, and Tall Child—make me feel pretty.

By sucking at sports, I actually improved in character. First, I became less self-conscious. Look at me all you like as I awkwardly attempt something out of my comfort zone. As long as I'm wearing lipstick and a strong bra, I am confident! Second, I can watch basketball, tennis, swimming, and track competitions and be entertained. I'm sports-educated; I can relate. I counted flags to avoid backstroking into a concrete wall. I waited nervously for a track pistol to send me sweating around a rosy rubber oval. I rode the basketball bench in popcorn warm gyms across Sevier County. Third, I don't mind working with people who are better than I am in some capacity. I admire success and talent and I don't mind pulling up the rear. Every team has a Flo-Jo and a Slo-Jo. Finally, I am not afraid to step outside the barn and try something abstract or seemingly out of reach. Tall Child and I got on a kick where we seriously discussed hiking the Appalachian Trail—until we realized that neither one of us can miss six months of work, we can't afford all the lodge and site fees, we have two children to raise, and we're terrified of heights. And black bears. And copperheads. And being rained on.

In the spirit of book research, I asked Tall Child, who coached youth basketball and baseball for many years, "As a coach, what is your attitude toward your worst player, someone like me?"

He answered, "I try to give him more attention than the others to make him feel like an important part of the team."

I asked, "What is your advice to that player who is on the team and not one bit of good?"

He answered, "Play hard and enjoy the game. Sports keep you from playing video games. They make you interact with other kids. You learn how to work with others. That's about it."

Oh, I think there's much more to learn than that, but I like Tall Child's outlook. In middle school, high school, and college, I finally did contribute to a team— not as an athlete, but as a musician who can forever brag that I played Division I.

Clarinet.

What's not to love, Peyton?

Theory 8: If you want the ultimate college experience, join the band.

Scales tests toughen you up. If you want the ultimate college experience, you must begin with scales. In fourth grade. What could be worse than straddling a clarinet and forcing air through the long plastic tube (because your parents can't afford a wooden one) and squawking a version of "Do-Re-Mi" in front of your peers? My guess is that, on a given day, band directors take more Tylenol than all other teachers combined, and that is saying a lot. While fourth, fifth, sixth, seventh, and eighth grade band classes are often a source of communal torture, they are also highlights of awkward middle school years.

One fellow instrumentalist hated middle school band so much he sat in the back row and chewed up an entire Trapper Keeper notebook in protest.

Basketball is important in all of East Tennessee, thanks to The University of Tennessee's legendary coach Pat Summitt and her champion Lady Vols, so my K-8 grade school, Pigeon Forge Elementary, held pep rallies for our Tiger and Lady Tiger basketball teams. The band played. Imagine a stack of slouching preteen goobers sporting tight moussed perms and Coca-Cola shirts. Imagine metal-clad-teeth clenching rented instruments. Imagine the sounds we produced: a sub-harmonic mix of gastric discomfort. Our short, yet popular playlist included the following songs:

"The Star Spangled Banner"
"Cheer Cheer" (Notre Dame)
"Eye of the Tiger"
"Rocky Top"
And our closer: "Tequila"

Delicious showed up ready to clap away at our first rally but left deflated; she said our version of "Rocky Top" sounded like a funeral dirge. What can I say? Young musicians are like English speakers in foreign countries: when we're unsure, we get loud and slow. Big Booty J taught at Pigeon Forge Elementary then. No joke: We closed every rally with "Tequila" and halfway through the song, BBJ strutted to the center of the gym floor and did the Pee-wee Herman dance. Within minutes, other teachers followed and the stands emptied. The entire student body broke it down, slowly, so the instrumentalists could stay together to fire up the Tigers and Lady Tigers. In 1987 and 1988, the Lady Tigers were 34 and 0. Just sayin'. In band there were basic rules we learned, and with a little imagination, these rules can translate to other parts of life:

- Don't play your instrument on the way to the band room.
- Stay ahead of the pain.
- Find a good alterations lady.
- Count your luggage and uniform pieces.
- Clean your spit valve.
- Wax your corks.

Speaking of wax, after the custodians polished our asbestos tile floors, several band boys liked to ruin the janitors' work. They set their hard instrument cases down on the shiny surface, paced several steps backward, and sprinted to dive onto the cases. Hair-gelled rat tails zipped by as boys rode their black cases, lightning speed, down the length of those buffed hallways to execute Big Wheel spin outs within inches of a concrete block wall. Custodians complained, so the boys would cover their tracks by rubbing their T-shirts across the skid marks to hide their trails. Friends, if you try this at home and you don't play brass, borrow a case from a friend who does. The ride is just not the same on a flute case.

Like any musician, I paid my middle school dues, but my high school band experience was better. I had my first big crush at Gatlinburg-Pittman High School band camp. Get your minds out of the gutter, *American Pie* fans, please —I am a teacher's daughter! I was nervous about high school in general and about marching and playing at the same time. But, as I met up with other band members in the G-P parking lot to board the cheese wagon to band camp at East Tennessee State University, I spotted a *key*-ute sophomore saxophone player. The heat waves floating from the August asphalt were nothing compared to the waves of anxiety that riddled my developing body. Let's just say I was more hormonal than harmonic. We flirted our way through band camp and even played pool together in the ETSU student center. Was that a date? All I remember is sucking at pool (of course) and hearing "Sweet Child o' Mine" on the rec room stereo.

Also that week, I tripped. Often. Finally, I looked down at my feet to see a Tretorn on the left and a Reebok on the right. Seven days at band camp with two different shoes.

On the way home, the sexy saxophonist and I sat together on the bus! We held hands! I guess the magic wore off between Johnson City and Gatlinburg because our romance never matured beyond band camp. Maybe he saw my shoes. Band crushes are the best because he is trapped with you—for hours—on a bus, in a band room, in a parade waiting line, or at a game.

Away games made me anxious. First, I was terrified I'd leave a piece of my instrument or uniform in Gatlinburg. Second, I had to ride with Otto the bus driver. I can't nickname him here. "Otto" is just too perfect. At South Doyle High School, lead-footed, farsighted Otto steered the band bus to scrape the entire side of our team's football bus. One day, the bus and the band inside were climbing the Smokies toward Clingman's Dome, the highest point on the Appalachian Trail, to cross into Cherokee, North Carolina, for a parade. The bus leaned hard to the right. I looked out the window to find my face parallel to the ground, only the ground was thousands of feet below, at the bottom of a ravine ... or as we say in the mountains, a gulley. Maybe all those geometrical stunts happened because Otto drove with his eyes on the rear-view mirror. All the way. For a reason.

There are always rumors about make-out sessions in the back of the bus. Innocent and terrified after being so cruelly dumped or forgotten by the sexy sax player and avoiding the gulley, I sat up front and kept my eyes on the horizon — and on Otto.

You meet a lot of characters when you're in the marching band. Bus drivers are one thing, but band directors are a different breed. They live on the edge of temper tantrums, the slightest bit of perversion, and borderline inappropriate commentary. If I had any musical talent, *I* might make a good band director.

My junior and senior years of high school, I was the drum major — maybe just because I could be trusted with the key to the band room. The tryouts were tough. I practiced for weeks, swinging my arms in 1 -2- 3- 4 rhythms and cut time to records of classical music, James Bond themes, and the "Oklahoma!" soundtrack. I counted time with my left hand and brought the invisible musicians to crescendo and decrescendo with my right, marching backward, rolling my feet, holding an authoritative stare.

The best parts of being drum major? One, no more duck walking to fast tempo Broadway theme songs for me. Two, I got to pick out a spicy *feminine* uniform. Still polyester, but girly. The first year, I chose a tuxedo jacket rimmed in gold with the shortest shorts I could wear. I did have to tolerate three pairs of support hose to stay warm and keep everything in the polyester. The second year, I wore a flouncy mini-skirt and gold sequined jacket. Awesome. Both years, I sported white leather band boots with tassels. There's just something about those boots. Tall Child, the cool jock, cracked up the first time he saw a photo of me in my boots. He just doesn't get band. Poor guy.

I loved high school band and all the people involved. Instead of hitting a post-graduation chalet party on Ski Mountain Drive in Gatlinburg, my band buddies and I hit our director's house. We adore the flawed but fabulous Music Man, and his lovely wife, Barefoot Nontessa (she's classy, but known for not cooking), for being such colorful characters of our youth.

Speaking of cool, years of scales, terrifying bus rides, and freezing my tail off in Gatlinburg, Music Man and high school band prepared me well for college band. I left behind the stadium where Delicious took up tickets and the beloved guidance counselor, Bo, sold his famous Bo Dogs in the concession stand. I entered UT's Neyland Stadium with its 107,000 screaming football fans. Subtract ten parent chaperones, add two state troopers. Swap one cheese wagon for seven chartered busses, baby! Our away games traded up, too—from Oneida and Oliver Springs, Tennessee, to The University of Georgia, The University of Florida, bowl games, and the Presidential Inaugural Parade in Washington, D.C. My middle-class buddies and I marched in front of the President of the United States of America! By the way, Al Gore has no rhythm. I saw it with my own eyes.

The bus rides could be tough, especially if I'd downed a little too much Southern Comfort the night before. Using the bus bathroom was as tricky a maneuver as an end zone flip turn. College co-eds can sleep anywhere. I usually sat up front to be first off at restaurants and stay as far away from the bathroom traffic as possible. But, sometimes I had to *go*. Band folks must be agile and considerate. We have our own ways. In a band bus carrying young growing boys and girls, some are wiped out from working and going to college, some are hung over, some are still drunk, and the majority are asleep at any given time, day or night, on each other, against arm rests, and often in the filthy floor. To get to the restroom, we crossed the narrow thirty-foot corridor by stepping on armrests and holding onto luggage racks. Even I, the uncoordinated clarinetist, managed not to land my size nine in an upper classman's abdomen. There were some close calls. When I met a restroom visitor on his or her return trip, we silently swapped foot placement on armrests and utilized strongholds on luggage racks for balance. This could be another good way to incite romance: when the boy you like goes to the bathroom, meet him on his return trip. Why did I just now think of that? Dang!

I was a better musician than athlete, but still just mediocre. I got so sick of my section leader, whom we called Mama, trying to privately tutor me that I announced to the clarinet squad, "I am tone deaf." Band geeks gasped. From then on, fellow clarinets treated me as a special needs musician. Perfect. I could focus on my real goal: having a good time on the UT athletic department's generous per diem. Cute boys at bars in Athens, Memphis, and Gainesville would inevitably ask, "Are y'all here for the game?"

I'd answer, "Yes, we are with the band."

The boys would ask, "What do you play?"

I'd answer, "Oh, I'm a majorette." Guys buy more drinks for twirlers than honkers. Plus, thanks to the sky-high stadium seats, I could get away with it. As far as they knew, I could be that hot feature twirler with fire batons.

I met my first real college boyfriend, a trombone player, at band camp. The magic of band love is unique. In full uniform, I used to tease him, "I'm naked beneath my clothes." He called me his "Orange Blossom Special." Speaking of nudity, band folks can't be modest. No locker rooms for band. Think fashion show models; add poundage, all putting on the same outfit. Use your band bus imagination.

I tried to date outside band, but it was tough. My Great Uncle G lived in a retirement home in Oregon. We wrote letters to each other. He talked about how the women fought to sit beside him on the van to Walmart. I wrote about classes and family. My sophomore year, he sent me a note with a newspaper clipping. The note read, "Bug, I read this article about a really nice boy at your school. I figured, since he is on the football team and you are in the band, you may get to know each other. He would be a good husband to catch!" I hated to tell Uncle G, though he did scamper by me in the end zone once as I waited to perform the half-time show, Peyton Manning never looked my way. I don't think ampersands and spats were his thing.

Speaking of being hot in a uniform, I was HOT. I packed Ziploc bags with ice and put them in my hat. My piccolo friend and I took turns chewing Double-Mint gum and blowing our minty fresh breath on the back of each other's necks to cool off. Try it. It works! Only an Appalachian Trail through hiker can relate to hours of sweltering heat and, after a rushed half-time performance, sucking down an ice-cold Coca-Cola. You *can* dance in hot wool, so might as well. Plus, the spats and plume just add to the dance flava. If you want to scare the heck out of a fellow band member, walk up to him/her right before step-off at an away game, fake a panicky look, and ask, "Where's your plume?"

Men in band can be impatient and uncensored, which is not what most people think. I loved yet feared my band director, The Legend. He was bold and honest. Once, at practice, he yelled through his microphone from his perch in a cherry-picker to a chunky piccolo player, "Girl on the 30-yard hash mark, move back! You are in front of the line. Well, hell, you're behind it, too!"

After a miserably wet, scorching hot defeat in Gainesville, we were on the band bus changing out of our stinky wool uniforms when a wasted male Gator fan, shouting profanities, tried to board our bus. Good thing Spits, a tuba player from Salina, was up front. The Gator made it up two steps before Spits punched him in the face so hard that the Gator did the Nestea Plunge onto the sidewalk.

Back to the state troopers. On another trip, the band stayed at a sprawling, one-story motor court. In every room, sliding glass doors framed a view of a grass lawn that contained a wide pond. We were out of the main town and not within walking distance of any place fun, so we created our own party strip. We room-hopped to socialize. A friend and I were hanging out in some brass players' room. One of the state troopers, a middle-aged round man, wobbled by the sliding glass door, on watch, to make sure we were behaving, when a trumpet player stated, "Look at that fat redneck strutting around like he's got control. He has no idea he just escorted marijuana across three state lines!"

No, I didn't smoke pot, but remember, musicians have risk-loving, creative souls. Many, if not most, world famous artists began their careers in folding metal chairs in middle school band rooms.

To this day, I get excited when I stand in charter bus exhaust fumes. My olfactory senses take me back to a carefree time when I had per diem on road trips, no serious job, and could convince others I was a majorette. I went on beach trips with three-hundred and fifty friends. I accompanied famous musicians like Lee Greenwood and the Atlanta Drum and Bugle Core. Like a real musician, I recorded

CDs and tapes that thrifty brass players sold, for a cut, in the upper decks, yelling "Band tapes!" I drank the coldest Coca-Colas. I swayed and played "The Tennessee Waltz" after every game. I snagged warm, leftover stadium dogs from metal carts on the way back to the band room, where we watched half-time video to see who all screwed up, just so we could harass them. I've been inside music, which means I enjoy it with an enlightened intensity. In other words, I experienced things through band that would never have experienced otherwise.

Go Band!

So, if you want a great education, go to a great university. If you want the ultimate college experience at that university, join the band. When Tall Child talks big about his days in juco basketball, I like to counter with this: "Look, only one person in this household played every football fall Saturday in front of 107,000 fans, witnessed multiple Navy fighter jet flyovers, and accompanied Lee Greenwood as he sang 'God Bless the USA.' Only one person in this house played Division I."

I spotted these boys on a smoke break.

Theory 9: Everyone should work in a restaurant.

Let's get down to business. Restaurant business. I grew up in tourist towns Gatlinburg, Pigeon Forge, and Sevierville, Tennessee. I know many people who enjoy successful careers in hospitality. I place high value on the innate lessons learned by serving the general public. Sharky and Gnome <u>will</u> work at *least* one summer in a restaurant. Why? Restaurant work offers an intense tutorial. I want my boys to experience the dining room: a place of social norms and cool, quiet protocol. I want them to experience the kitchen. They need to witness the impossible possibility of uniforms in chaotic yet choreographed movement. They need to inhale the pungent combo of old grease, chopped onions, and bleach. They should hear pots and pans fight scalding water in Hobart dishwashing machines. I want them to hear and overcome the dead-on, efficient, sometimes perverse, yet truly funny language of the restaurant nation. I hope they can memorize and deliver. I want my boys to get so mad and so stressed that they slam cork-lined trays into metal so hard they test swinging kitchen door hinges. I want them to rally and recover, in public. Most of all, I want them to serve others.

Restaurants are labs of bacteria, behavior, conflict, passion, composure, language, class warfare, and comedy. Sharky and Gnome come from a long line of restaurant workers. After I share with you what those in my crowd experienced and learned, you'll either dine at home or tip twenty percent, no matter what the service is like.

So, what should my boys expect to learn when they work in a restaurant?

1. They'll learn a new language. Due to necessary haste and aversion to waste, kitchen folks use a short-hand tongue to communicate with one another. Curious? Sit at any Waffle House counter. The language is as universal as the American dollar. Here's a short list of terms with definitions. Dang, I do love a glossary!

86'd – taken off the menu

Rush – a pile of customers coming in at once

Walking out – just what it sounds like. Dishwashers and line cooks love to threaten this and actually do it!

Two, four, six, etc., "top" – number of places at a table

Got sat – a warning issued by another waitress, as in "you just got sat a four-top"

On the fly – indicates the cook better hurry with that dish

On the square – means four of whatever food item
Side work – the nasty stuff servers do after closing (vacuum, refill salt & pepper shakers, wash syrup bottles, mop, clean out the salad bar)

Crumb Pickers – children

E.P.'s – extra plates or children who order extra plates

Charger – the fancy plate under the regular plate

Expeditor – the 15-year-old or the panicky manager who takes food off the line and arranges it on trays for the servers

Nuke – microwave (comes in handy when you forget to bake the potatoes)

Cow – the giant milk dispenser

Pearl Diver – the dishwasher (the person, not the Hobart machine)

2. They'll learn that lewd language and vile references are part of life's experiences. So they'll get over it and not walk around waiting to be offended.

I was 20, looking good, and looking to make some solid summer money. My Applewood Farmhouse Restaurant manager Zero was a diminutive guy from the Middle East. He had bad manners. He forced me to start out as a hostess even though I had experience as a breakfast waitress at IHOP. Zero stood, quite smugly, at eye-level to my space heaters and liked to taunt me by dangling the carrot of a lucrative waitress position. Some of his first words to me were, "What size uniform do you need, a *large* in the top?"

My summer serving at IHOP was my favorite stint. When I asked for hot syrup, the line cooks responded, "Oh, you like it hot?"

When I yelled over the serving line to beg cooks to change an order, guys would harass, "We knew you were a screamer!"

When the ice scoop hit metal, a waitress would ask for more ice. In East Tennessee, "ice" is pronounced "eis" or "aes" so the cooks would yell back, "Oh, I'll give you some whenever you're ready!"

My cousin Moon, then a teacher, worked summers at the Heidelberg Restaurant on top of Ski Mountain Road, at touron favorite Ober Gatlinburg. The place had a polka band, German cuisine, and a tram shuttle to and from downtown Gatlinburg. Moon is good-looking. He yelled an order of Bratwurst across the line and a stout, greasy-haired, seasoned fraulein cook yelled back, "Take off 'em clothes and jump up on 'is here table. I'll show ye some Bratwurst!"

3. My boys will learn the art of nepotism.

Delicious told me she once worked with this guy whose daddy owned the restaurant that employed her. The boy constantly griped at the staff. Once, he yapped at a kitchen worker who had plated a juicy dessert for himself, "You can't eat that pie! My dad would be very upset." The worker stuck his thumb in the pie and said, "Oh, well, it's damaged now." By summer's end, the kitchen help, sick of the boy's incessant bull, ganged up on him, soaked cathead biscuits in water, and hurled them at him. For you Yankees, cathead biscuits are named such because the biscuits' depth and circumference match that of any old Tom cat wallerin' around in the Southern dust.

At Country Kitchen Restaurant I waited on the owner's teenage daughter and her companions. She asked for an extra side of green beans. I informed her that she'd incur an extra charge. She said, "Did you know that my dad, *your boss*, signs your paycheck?"

I said, "Yes. Did *you* know that I'm going to tell him his daughter was rude to his employee? Extra sides are $1.75."

4. Sharky and Gnome will recognize and appropriately deal with favoritism.

I hated being a hostess at Applewood Farmhouse Restaurant. Why? Because when my uppity co-hostesses found out I was a virgin, they harassed me, endlessly. Restaurants aren't the most virginal environments. Anyway, at this restaurant, my daddy's old, old friend G.G. was the head cook. As he flipped, filleted, and fried, he watched the abuse I suffered and got as mad as a hornet at those snooty girls. If waitresses and hostesses wanted lunch, we had to ask G.G. to cook it for us. Cooks cuss — blatantly. They are hot, worn out, stressed out, and often frustrated. One day two of these girls and I landed on the line for lunch at the same time. G.G. babied me. "Bug, let me fix you something good. How about a ribeye, baked potato, and salad?" The girls whined, "What!?! You said we could only have grilled cheese. Why does she get a steak?"

G.G. answered with authority, "Because she is my girl and y'all are bitches."

To avoid the hateful hostesses, I often volunteered to fill in in the kitchen—as a fritter fryer, salad girl, or dessert girl. Plus, I loved sweating through eight fast hours in the raucous, comical kitchen. This crazy little guy everyone called Animal was our main pearl diver. I think he was named after some Muppet character. Animal was short and scrawny, low on teeth, and high on energy. He wore the same pink T-shirt and denim overalls every single day. Animal braided his long, reddish blonde hair down his back like Willie Nelson. (Hair is the enemy in the restaurant business. Mine was long too, so I wore it in a French braid.) Animal was my friend. He begged me all the time, "Bug, let's go out back after 'er shift's up and let 'er braids out. I swar' mah hair's longer 'an yourn." Animal was not fit for the customers' spaces, but every now and then he got curious. He slid through the kitchen door and pranced among polished tables and chairs. Immediately, a waitress would spot him and command, "Animal! Get back in the kitchen!"

5. Restaurant work will teach Sharky and Gnome that mistakes happen. They'll learn to suck it up.

Never dip your ass in ice. You <u>never</u> dip ice with a glass because if the glass breaks, there's glass in the ice. The moron who used glass in ice then has to empty the entire bin, and then be forced to yell "We need more ice!" to the line cooks. Big Booty J learned this the hard way. She toted a round tray loaded with filled water glasses through the dining room at Green Valley Restaurant in Pigeon Forge. Her right, thick-soled waitress shoe landed on a pat of butter.

She landed in a split. Her tray of water glasses went airborne, crashing into the salad bar of chopped iceberg, olives, cheese, and pickled beets. She had to clean and restock the whole bar.

Machines are designated for certain tasks. One waitress learned this the hard way at IHOP. On a diet, she squirted skim milk from the cow into a metal cup and tossed in a scoop of Slim-Fast. All I remember is hearing her scream, "Oh, no! Sorry sorry sorry!" and watching the entire waitress station and its inhabitants get sprayed with pellets of chocolate Slim-Fast. Those milkshake blenders are meant for hard-packed ice cream, not milk and diet powders.

Look behind you. Delicious once witnessed a co-waitress catch her toe coming out of the walk-in cooler. She tripped forward, dumping five gallons of homemade Roquefort dressing down the front of the maître d's white leisure suit. If you pay attention, you'll hear servers whisper to one another, "Behind you," to ward off impending catastrophe.

The show must go on. My cousin Mooch, an elementary school teacher and sister to Moon, waitressed a summer with Delicious at Applewood Farmhouse Restaurant. Perhaps Mooch over-snacked on fritters or gobbled down too much of the greasy beans; Mooch had an "accident" underneath her calico floor-length, mountain woman waitress costume. She tossed her panties, cleaned up, scalded her hands, and went back to work. Hours later, she and Delicious stood in the Sunroom, which boasted a giant birdcage of finches and floor to ceiling windows. Mooch quipped, "Hey Delicious, look at this!" She spread her legs and overdramatized her efforts to Windex the glass. Delicious saw the entire outline of Mooch's cooch.

6. My boys have to learn that we all have clients, those clients can be really obnoxious, and we have to cope.

I realize that there may come a time when Sharky and Gnome want to rip off the apron and walk out. I know. I "stuck it to the man" a few times. Yes, kitchen managers and co-workers can make you crazy, but the customers, oh, the customers can make you mad enough to spit. Or quit. And by the way, despite the common saying, they are not always right — typically, they are flat out wrong.

Restaurant nation, feel free to finish this sentence, "Servers hate when customers _____." I share the following on your behalf:

- Parents who croon to disinterested children, "Tell the lady what you want." It's obnoxious, especially when you hear it twenty times in one shift. Plus, don't we already know the crumb picker wants chicken tenders?

- Customers who look at the menu and say, "Decisions, decisions." Stop trying to convince everyone you can quote a president or theorist. Just decide.

- People who order decaf. What is the point? Do you swim in your socks? I bet the same folks fish in waders and eat Egg-Beaters and turkey burgers. Wimps.

- People who order extra lemons, squeeze them pulpless into a water glass, and stir in ten packets of sweetener. That *ain't* lemonade. You *are* a tightwad.

- Vinegar and oil. We all know you are trying to act sophisticated in front of your friends. Admit it, you really want some good old ketchup and mayonnaise, a.k.a. Thousand Island dressing. Plus, that's the same oil we use in the deep fryer and the same vinegar we use to clean the coffee maker. Bon appétit!

- Customers who run the waiters to death. Don't get all "lord of the manor" on us. By the way, these people are consistently the worst tippers. Interesting dynamic, don't you think?

- Breakfast customers who don't tip fifteen percent or more, just because it's breakfast time. Breakfast servers wait on twice as many customers, carry twice as many dishes, and make half the money. Show some respect.

- Customers who discuss the tip or the service with the server. So degrading. You will never hear a server say, "You did a good job ordering quickly and eating all your chili-cheese nachos."

- Non-tippers, a.k.a. stiffers – you suck. You just never know what that server is dealing with personally or in the kitchen. Err on the side of kindness. A waitress who worked at Heidelberg with Delicious became irate after a big table of tourons stiffed her. She chased them out of the restaurant, through Ober Gatlinburg, all the way to the tram station. Just before the tram doors slid shut, she flung foul language and their pocket-change into the tram and said, "Here, you need this more than I do!"

7. Sharky and Gnome will learn how to QUIT.

There's only so much one can take in the restaurant business. So if Sharky and Gnome have to toss their aprons, they can learn from their familial predecessors how to do it with flair.

My uncle Mule was the general manager of a pancake house for a few years. When he quit, he just showed up unannounced on his day off and quipped, "Hey, I just came by to pick up my paycheck and tell you that yesterday is my last day."

Zero's pervy moves got old, so I decided to ditch the job. My college sweetheart, a huge Richard Nixon fan, coached me on how to confront Zero. After my shift I went to tiny Zero's tiny office and announced, "I am quitting. You are dishonest. You can't talk to women the way you do. This is America. You don't have Bug to kick around anymore."

BBJ, at age eighteen, began her first shift at Howard Johnsons in Gatlinburg. As she puts it, "a table full of Yankees ordered ice cream *sodas*." Being from Columbus, Georgia, the Deep South, she had no clue what an ice cream *soda* was. Instead of attempting the impossible task of making the Yankee dessert, she deserted. She sprinted out the back door into the Smoky Mountain mist.

8. If they don't know how to quit, my boys will learn how to get fired.

Another summer, BBJ, madly in love with townie stud Gravy (who is now my exceptional uncle), waitressed at The Wagon Wheel, known to locals as "The Spoke." BBJ called in sick one Friday and showed up for her Saturday shift with a motorcycle windburn, ski-boat sunburn, and Budweiser head burn as a result of her "sick day" with Gravy. A fellow waitress met her at the door and said, "Thar ain't no use you comin' in here. You done got canned."

When business is slow, servers get mischievous. One college summer, a bored Delicious and waitress friend grabbed a plus-sized co-worker, slid open the beer cooler, and pushed her down into the frozen box. Her plump rear was wedged between metal sliding doors and ice-cold beer. She, the victim, was giggling so hard she couldn't climb out. Delicious and her cohort took on the challenge of seeing how much crushed ice they could throw up the girl's pencil skirt, from across the kitchen. All three got caught. All three got fired.

Trout washed dishes at Hobies in Gatlinburg, where workers could eat free from a limited menu. But my uncle couldn't resist the fried Rainbow Trout, off limits to staff. Sneaky and good-looking, he sweet-talked a waitress into forging an order every night at the end of his pearl-diving shift. Each evening, he wrapped the plated contraband delicacy in aluminum foil, grabbed silverware, and slid home to enjoy his meals.

By summer's end he had twelve place settings of Hobies dinnerware, the nickname "Trout," and a pink slip.

9. My boys could learn how to fall in love at a restaurant.

Yes, the band bus is hot and heavy, but there's something special about summer kitchen chaos. As you've probably gathered, Delicious, a UGA graduate-turned-English teacher, fled Georgia in late May in the summers of 1965-1971 to hustle tables in numerous eateries in the arts and crafts community of Gatlinburg. She admits she was far from professional, and her main goals were to make enough tips to buy a twin-pack of Ruffles potato chips and a twelve-pack of Budweiser every night. She'd wrap up her side work around 11 p.m. and crowd into a car with crushes and friends and head to Newfound Gap parking lot to drink, eat, flirt, and watch the spectacular Smoky Mountain hot pink, purple, blue and gold sunrise.

The course of humanity was altered when the meat grinder at Steak & Lobster broke down. On July 3, 1972, in the kitchen at Howard's Restaurant, Delicious (five foot ten, lean, with a shag haircut and a summer creek tan) sashayed with her drink tray into the kitchen and saw a blonde, curly headed boy with wire-rimmed glasses and a cigarette hanging from his mouth, its ashes a half-inch long and falling into the hamburger meat he was grinding. He worked at Steak & Lobster and had to borrow equipment at Howard's.

She said, "What's your name? I've never seen you before." Taken by surprise, he sheepishly squeaked out his full name. His nickname growing up was Pot, because he stayed outside and was filthy as a little boy. His nickname in Gatlinburg summers was Smoke. Strange coincidence.

The cooks told Smoke, "She is warm for your form and hot for your bod." They also told Smoke that Delicious had a wild streak, which was not true. Like me, Delicious's outgoing personality and upper attributes often disappointed men.

In great anticipation, the next time Delicious swung open the kitchen doors to pick up a sizzling platter of steaks, a fired-up Smoke asked Delicious, "Would you like to go for a Jeep ride tomorrow morning?"

She said, "Sure!"

September 16, the madly in love Smoke and Delicious got married. Two years later they welcomed their first child: me! Delicious re-nicknamed Smoke the more parentally appropriate name Pooh.

Tall Child missed his chance at restaurant work. He was too busy shooting free throws and wearing sweater vests, I guess. So, I like to enlighten him as we dine. His manners are superb, thankfully. One table-made lemonade episode during our courtship and I would have 86'd him on the fly.

I listened to J-Bird and Dogwood Deb argue the merits of public school vs. private school. Finally, J-Bird asked me, a *teacher* at that time, "Don't you think children learn more about life in a rougher public school instead of being in a private school bubble?"

I responded, "Well, there are great public schools and terrible private schools. Give your child the safest, most intellectually challenging school—public or private—that you can afford. If you want her to learn walks of life and FACTS of life, give her one summer of restaurant work.

Sharky got a taste of the retail restaurant when his baseball team held a pancake breakfast at a local Chili's. He had to *wash his hands* and show up at 7 a.m. to serve brave diners, a.k.a. smitten grandparents. Two hours into his shift, I looked to see this:

I should have yelled, "Animal, get back in the kitchen!"

For many years after I left the restaurant business, I missed the unique opportunity to demonstrate grace under fire. But, thanks to Sharky's athleticism, I have new venues in which to strive for self-control while squelching sarcasm and asinine behavior — basketball gyms and baseball parks.

Gnome consoles Tall Child after umpires
kick Tall Child off the baseball field.

Theory 10: In youth sports, parents are the real performers.

When Sharky, age five, debuted in tee ball, I hoped the athleticism that runs in my family would skip a generation and shine. At Sharky's first game, a batter knocked a bullet off the tee into the infield, and Sharky snatched the ball from the air. Out! What a stud! I was elated, until the coach gave a different boy the game ball. I complained to Delicious, who counseled, "Bug, if you're going to watch your child play sports, you're going to have to get control of yourself."

Uncle Trout told Tall Child, "If you want Sharky to get a fair shake in sports, you have to coach him."

I vowed to watch my mouth. Tall Child signed up to coach multiple sports in the local youth league.

Sharky has played in at least two hundred baseball games and what seems like a thousand basketball games since then. I try to stay composed, but even the most well-mannered mama and papa bears fall a few links backward in evolution when our cubs are under pressure or "mistreated." We've got scoreboards for the kiddos, but parents' behavior is hard to track. I thank my crowd for contributing to this Theory and for helping me come up with a label for each type of extreme sports parent. Descriptions are fairly general to avoid identification. I mean, we are talking about teachers, preachers, social workers, doctors, bankers, repairmen, and accountants. Reader, which of these high performing parents are you?

Make-the-Mosters

My friend Baton Swiper reminded me about a couple of over-zealous moms who created NBA level excitement in their sons' three-on-three basketball league. You see, Baton Swiper and I bought a huge role of butcher paper. Each week, we ripped off a giant rectangle and graciously wrote all the players' names (from our team AND the opposing team) on the paper. After a pre-game bathroom break, the little boys lined up. On cue, Baton Swiper's husband, Trombone Stud, hit play on her ghetto blaster. The boys ripped through the paper onto the basketball court, took opposing sides, and shot pregame layups to "Rocky Top" and an old ESPN "Jock Jams" cassette.

Some parents probably thought we were nuts, but some of *their* boys will never run through paper again. In one of our last games, I said to the other team's coach, who looked unhappy—probably because we'd beaten him three times already, "Hey, we're going to line up to run through the paper in about two minutes."

He pouted, "My team will NOT be running through your paper!"

Hint: If you do the paper thing, be sure to poke holes. Remember, I was not a cheerleader past kindergarten. When Sharky did a practice run at home, his then forty-four-pound body hit that banner with full force, and with equal force bounced backward into the wall.

Speaking of music, my aunt Terrific carried a boom box to her daughter A-Boo's preppy yet fierce Yummyville School softball games. For eight straight years. Terrific played antagonistic song selections, including Queen's "Another One Bites the Dust." Years later, A-Boo played collegiate golf at Vanderbilt. During her sophomore year she was paired against a University of Alabama player at a golf tournament in Athens, Georgia. Through several holes of small talk, A-Boo and the Bama golfer realized they both played high school softball. A-Boo said, "Yeah, I played for Yummyville School."

The Bama golfer explained, "Oh, lord, that's the team with that OBNOXIOUS Boom Box Lady!"

Outliers

They sit alone way down the first base line or they stand in the gym corner. Maybe they're nervous, maybe they're focused on the game, and maybe they're doing some intense one-on-one parent-child coaching. Or, maybe they just don't want to hear the women in the bleachers swap recipes. Sorry, guys.

Budgeteers

Gate passes, three-dollar nachos, gas, weekends in Holiday Inn Express hotels, and Gatorades add up fast. Why not tuck your body between a cooler, a bat bag, and a stadium throw in the back of your SUV? Don't breathe. And, once you are in, don't leave.

On-The-Road-Off-Duty Parents

These are parents, typically fathers, who forsake normal supervisory responsibilities on road trips. Post-match, they crowd the hotel lobby to imbibe beer and rehash game highlights while their children mistreat elevators, vandalize hotel exercise facilities, and ding-dong-ditch unfortunate second floor neighbors. It amazes me how Sharky could play three intense basketball games in one day, swim for an hour, then walk on a treadmill in the Comfort

Suites workout room. Why is it that unsupervised young athletes gravitate toward exercise rooms?

Off duty parents hemorrhage money. The players score solid bling like Phiten necklaces, tourney T-shirts, sunglasses, and expensive beef jerky. Hung-over daddies don't argue in front of concession stands. They peel out the dollars and say, "Get me a Gatorade while you're up there."

I once asked my buddy, Mason-Dixon, a Northern-born woman with a Southern disposition, who was obviously worn out from keeping up with four children at an out of town tourney in suffocating humidity, "Where are your little ones?"

She sighed, "They are either on the playground or in a stranger's van half-way to Michigan."

Rule Freaks

Rule Freaks are those parents who are, as Terrific likes to say, "often wrong, but never in doubt." Rule Freaks like to second-guess the umpires, forgetting that different age groups and leagues have different rules. Rule freaks also question players' ages, as in "That boy cann*ot* be eleven-years-old and be that tall." When his mama is six-feet-four-inches tall and looks like an Auburn linebacker, *yes,* he can be that tall.

Lobbyists

Lobbyist parents kiss up to the coach, sweet-talk the coach's wife, and criticize other players, hoping to get their children more playing time. As a coach's wife, I like these parents because they bring the snacks. Bringing snacks is a pain.

Paranoid Schizophrenics

Some parents are convinced their children are about to get cut. There's so much at stake: college scholarships, draft day excitement, the NBA/NFL lifestyle, and paying off the re-re-re-refinanced mortgage! They are the parents who sign their children up for agility training. If the child sits out a quarter or an inning, these parents become intensely quiet and nervous, or whisper to one another in skeptical alliance. But, when their children hit RBIs or swish buzzer-beaters, they high-five and test their bras and belts with vigorous middle-aged jumping jacks, as if to say, "YES! There *is* a chance we'll be debt-free someday!"

Worriers

Worriers are typically mothers who squeal and gasp every time their angels foul hard, collide, or go full-speed coast-to-coast toward a backboard and the wall behind it. Worriers run onto the court and enter the dugout. Not cool, according to Sharky, so as a Worrier, I instead yell loudly from the stands, "Sharkeeeeeeeeee, are you okay?" Then I yell to the referees, "We don't want to go to Children's Hospital!" Worriers hand deliver sports drinks to their children during games. Also not cool, according to Sharky, so I send Gnome, who usually just drops the drink and runs because he's terrified of refs. Then, I send an older child to tell Sharky there's a drink on the bench for him. Geez. It's so much mental work keeping Sharky safe and hydrated.

Space Hogs

Some of us have back problems, okay? We get good comfy spots on the top bleachers where we can lean, or we find shady spots behind sandy backstops. Both are relaxing, and we score great views. Why should we leave just because our team isn't playing again for two hours? If you want to see the mother of the super athlete with innate competitive drive, just scan the backstop, or the top bleacher. Just *try* to get her to move.

Out-of-Touchers

Listen folks, when your child plays a sport, he or she is committed to a team. Period. Ask any old-school coach. Don't miss practice or games for birthdays, parties, or trips.

Gnome played tee ball, and Tall Child was the coach. As the coach's wife, it was my inherent duty to get trophies. Well, we had seven players every game I attended, so, I bought seven At the final game, we had eight players. Say what?!? I had to rush home to desperately search in a frenzy for an old Sharky trophy that looked like the ones I had bought for Gnome's team. Miraculously, I found one! I sped back to the game, just as the children were lining up to say, "Good game. Good game." Whew. Naturally, my child (who never missed a practice or an inning) had to sacrifice. I ordered another trophy for Gnome the next week and replaced Sharky's old trophy to its rightful dust-collecting position. What a pain. Who was that eighth player?

My dear friend, Ole Miss Glamour Girl (OMGG) once interrupted baseball practice because she had dinner reservations. Here's how it went down between her and our coach, The Best:

> OMGG yelled from the behind the fence across the field to second base to her son: "Phenom get your stuff."
> **The Best yelled back: "What?!? No!"**
> OMGG: "We have to leave!"
> **The Best: "WHY?"**
> OMGG: "We have dinner reservations!"
> **The Best: "It's Tuesday!"**
> OMGG: "It's Cinco De Mayo!"
> **The Best: "You're not *Mexican*!"**

Now, OMGG knows how to have a good time, but she doesn't know sports stuff. When we played near our neighborhood, she organized team tailgates complete with sandwich platters, adult juice boxes, tablecloths, and flowers. She mastered the *Southern Living* tailgate in her time at the iconic Grove at The University of Mississippi. She actually commented, "How can that umpire tell if it's a ball or a strike? He's standing *behind* the catcher!" OMGG didn't stop her criticism there. Regarding her son, she asked, "Why do people keep saying Phenom plays second base? He plays *between* first and second base." The first time she heard players and fans yell, "Three up, three down!" OMGG asked, "Why do they keep saying that? What does that even mean?"

Annoyers

Male coaches don't need to touch their privates. I know things in uniform itch but deal with it. I once warned Tall Child, "If that coach adjusts himself *down there* again, I will grab baby Gnome's Desitin out of the diaper bag and side-arm it toward the coach's cup."

Delicious says, "You should never hate anyone." Well, too bad. I *hate* the lady who shook a plastic bottle full of coins for an entire baseball game in Orlando, Florida. I complained to the concession stand manager. Her response? "I'm in food."

Grandparents

Speaking of hyper grannies, Delicious and Tall Child's mother Bop aren't fans of the bunt. Even if Sharky is zero for twelve three weekends in a row, they are one hundred percent certain he can hit a grand slam if only the coach will give the signal.

Pouters

These are parents and Daddy Ball Coaches who stomp off the field after a loss and say, "Get your bag." One Daddy Ball Coach refused—for two seasons—to give Tall Child the "good game" hand shake. Not even a fist bump. His bad attitude and poor sportsmanship just made beating him that much better.

Division 1's

These parents have genetic confidence and nothing to prove (no vicarious ambition) as they were successful in their own glory days. They know the rules, so they don't argue. They are tall, so they don't fight for the top bleacher or backstop seats. Umps recognize their frames and gaits as "having been there" and give them the cool-rod nod. The Best told a riveting story of one of his many teen victories. I asked, "How do you remember such detail?"

He said, "The older I get, the better I was."

Snappers

No one is immune. My kind-hearted, philanthropic sister-in-law Dogwood Deb became irate after her sweet nephew Sharky lost a tense baseball battle to Sumner County. No doubt cheated by refs, we exited in defeat while the winners cheered loudly on the way to their cars. Dogwood Deb lost her cool and screamed across the parking lot, "Oh, shut up and go back home to *Slum*ner County!"

After one baseball game, I saw a woman freak out so hard I expected to see her leave in a straight jacket. She screeched and thrashed like a wild animal. Luckily, she was inside the scorekeeper's chain-link protective box. She was in a cage rage.

At the end of a basketball game, I watched in horror as a granny went postal on her grandson. She kept yelling, "You look at me when I'm talkin' to you!" He couldn't. She had A & P eyes (one faced the Atlantic, the other the Pacific—the murky one).

Some of these heckling parents harass the coaches, the referees, the other teams' coaches, the other teams' fans, **and** *their own children*. I save my commentary for Tall Child for the car ride home. IF, IF, *IF* I ride home with him. You should see how he mistreats my super-athletic, often misunderstood Sharky when my baby misses free-throws. I never got that kind of treatment in the band!

Trout over-heckled the refs at one of cousin Roscoe's college basketball games, and the refs said, "You are out of here! Leave this gym!" Trout pointed at himself, and mouthed, "Me?" He'd driven a long way to watch Roscoe and was not about to leave. So, he faked them out and sneaked up to the balcony seats. He ducked in and out of the crowd to avoid being caught. It was like watching human Whack-A-Mole.

In the stands, I always keep an ear out for new, awesome one-liners. Often, passionate parents display an entertaining flash of bravado and wit. In the safe cloud of fan noise, we scream out mean things we'd never say anywhere else. Once, a frustrated Tall Child yelled up at me, "Your son sucks!"

I yelled back, "You suck!"

When we got home, Sharky and I banished Tall Child to the bedroom for the rest of the night.

So, as your child winds up to pitch, steps back in the pocket to throw, or sets up his shot, answer this question: How do you perform? Are you civilized in the shadows, or does the wild animal in you come out to play?

Of course they are.

Theory 11: The more a zoo advertises a critter, the less likely visitors are to actually see that critter.

Speaking of wild animals, let's talk about zoos. My training as a school teacher truly sharpened my ability to criticize pretty much anything, including things I know little about. I like to entertain Sharky and Gnome on a dime in the summers. Luckily, we live very close to Great Smoky Mountains National Park and The University of Tennessee—budget friendly attractions. But, when my beautiful, sweet niece Balloon Girl came to visit for a week from our state's capital, I had to step up my game. I took Sharky, Gnome, and Balloon Girl trudging through my Appalachian home place, The

Crippled Beagle Farm. We caught lightning bugs in our front yard. We bowled at The University of Tennessee's student center. But Balloon Girl had souvenir money to burn, so I had to find a gift shop before she returned to Nashville. Where is a great place to see stuff and spend money? The zoo!

Or, is it?

I *love* the local zoo. I've visited several animal-themed parks, petting exhibits, fairs, and zoos in my life, but, for my town's size, the local zoo reigns supreme. It is clean, convenient, well-managed, and the animals enjoy spacious habitats. "Habitat" is what you call cages and pens with synthetic rocks and fake tropical waterfalls to convince the animals that they are in Thailand, not Tennessee.

The only disturbing *animal* thing I ever saw at the zoo was a fifty-pound Aldabran Tortoise stuck on his back. He paddled away, hustling for friction and a flip. His scaly claws fought for naught. Within moments, a zoo employee rescued him. The second worst thing I ever saw at the zoo was when Sharky, then age four, escaped his rented stroller by unbuckling himself. I said something like, "Let's go see the lions!" He furiously unsnapped his safety belt and zoomed like a bullet down the path. But, he tripped, went airborne, and soared into a mound of black dusty mulch. He was a Southern Ground Hornbill.

The best animal at our zoo was old Tonka. He was an African elephant and I could count on seeing him. The second-best exhibit at the zoo is Dippin' Dots, the world's coldest ice cream. No matter what month it is when I go to the zoo, the day is hot. After I tromp around a 50+ acre hilly farm pretending I'm in Africa and see that Brazilian Rainbow Boa glassed in a humid box, the power of suggestion gives me hot flashes, so I cool off with frozen ball bearings of Cookies-n-Cream.

I once heard "Fox News" anchor Brian Kilmeade ask, "Why do people keep making pandas have more pandas?" I can tell you why, Brian. Supply for demand. Zoos advertise exotic visitors (animals they rent or borrow from other zoos) to ramp up visitation, but most folks just hear the ad or see the billboard in passing and think the animals have made a home in the local habitat. Not so. How many of you have been lured into the zoo, to the tune of $19.95 for adults and $17.95 for children over the age of two to see a critter from another part of the world, only to spend, sweat, and never lay eyes on the exotic creature?

The more a zoo advertises a critter, the less likely visitors are to actually see that critter. I've thought so for a long time, but I refuse to stop my safari. So, Balloon Girl, Sharky, Gnome, and I headed to the zoo. Balloon Girl is not a fan of hot uphill hiking, but when I told her about the gift shop, she perked up and grabbed her change purse from Gnome's stroller. We saw black bears recline, penguins waddle, and Tonka scoop water with his trunk. We looked through a huge habitat for the Western lowland gorillas but found only one. Another large gorilla rested inside a concrete structure. Sharky didn't like that environment and said, "He is miserable."

I said, "He is fine."

Sharky argued, "Really? Check out the look on his face."

I'm no Jane Goodall, but Sharky had a point. Sometimes I think animals are smarter than humans. They don't trip. They don't resist nature. They lie in the shade and refresh themselves with water. We humans eat hot nachos and hoof it up hills. We gawk. They yawn. Who is watching whom here? I've never heard a zoo lion roar, but I'm sure those lions have heard plenty of mamas yell.

As my little wards gazed upon the grassland zebras, Balloon Girl squished up her face and asked, "Aunt Bug, can we go to another part of the zoo. It stinks over here. Ewww, what is that smell?"

I explained in great, ahem, detail, "Zebra sh*t."

We migrated over to the baboon cage. Again, "Aunt Bug, it stinks over here, too! What is *that* smell?"

"Baboon sh*t."

FYI – Teachers aren't the most patient summer babysitters.

Two hours, two fruit slushies, and two plastic animal toys in, Sharky said, "Let's go to the other side."

Balloon Girl cried, "There's another side?"

"Yes! We have to go see the white alligator! I heard about it on the news!"

I was hot and tired, too, but I wanted to get the best bang for my buck, especially since that money should have gone toward the light bill. Balloon girl and I rallied when we saw the Dippin' Dots stand and took a much-needed break. Ahhh. Cool, refreshing, summertime ice cream. I could never eat meat at the zoo. Who could eat chicken nuggets while watching a bird show? Delicious hasn't eaten a hamburger since the time she pattied ground beef and looked out her kitchen window to see a cow, fifteen feet away, make its own patty.

Restored by our freezing cold sweet treat, we set out to see the white alligator on the far side of the 56-acre zoo. Halfway there, Balloon Girl, who was pushing Gnome in the stroller, stopped and gasped, "Oh my gosh, Aunt Bug, what time is it?"

I answered, "3:30. Why?"

She exclaimed, "Oh no! I am missing a show I really wanted to watch."

I asked, "What show?"

She answered, "It's a show about wild animals on Nickelodeon."

What'chu talkin' 'bout, Willis?

I said, "Balloon Girl! There's a rhinoceros forty feet in front of you!"

I later laughed with Delicious about the exchange and she said Balloon Girl was onto something—air conditioning and good editing. She could snack in comfort and be guaranteed a quality animal performance of roaring, fighting, killing, and cute baby critter cuddling. TV shows feature active animals, not yawners.

Some critters did perform for us. Gnome hooted as he watched North American River Otters dive, flip, and splash. I can always count on lemurs. Anywhere animals are on display, lemurs abound. Aren't they rodents? I thought they were almost extinct. Does it appear to you that all animals are "on the verge of extinction?" Uncle Trout caught a diamond back rattlesnake, and A-Boo released it to the other side of their farm because rattlesnakes are a protected species in Alabama. How about protecting *my* species, A-Boo?

So, off we went to the petting zoo to brush fat goats. Then to Kids Cove, a sweet little artificial creek bed where Gnomes can mimic their new river otter friends as their worn-out mamas rest in rocking chairs. The playground looked spotless, but when I saw goat-brushing, breast-feeding, nacho eating, and a sign reading "Children who are not potty-trained must wear swim diapers" in one panoramic view, I got totally grossed out. I packed up my crew and said, "Let's see this dang white alligator and get out of here."

Guess what. He wasn't there! A zoo attendant explained, "We just sent him to another zoo up North."

Uh-huh. Sure you did.

On the way home, I asked Gnome, who appeared to love the day, "What was your *faaaaaa*vorite animal at the zoo today?"

With certainty and excitement, he announced, "The whale!"

Really? I paid $17.95 for him to imaginarily see the most impossible animal to contain in a zoo? Next time, we're going to PetSmart to "see" a whale. It's much cheaper, and I can pick up dog food while I'm there.

When we got home, I was stilled miffed about the MIA white gator. I asked Tall Child, "What do you think about the zoo?"

He answered, "I don't."

Sharing the road.

Theory 12: Bicycle guys are selfish & make other people late for work.

Delicious cautioned me not to write this Theory because (and she is probably right) I will certainly offend some folks by griping about bicycle guys. I like to criticize in detail, so let me be specific so as to identify the "bicycle guys" about whom I complain. They are *not* the men and women who ride in parks and on back roads, on weekends or at night, for exercise or pleasure. I actually have several friends who bike for sport. I love to see their scenic Facebook and Instagram photos from atop Smoky Mountain overpasses. They are not the college students who choose frugal speed and efficient parking with bikes vs. cars. They *are* the guys who ride bicycles at rush hour, on the road, in school zones, in the way, and make us all nervous and late.

Hustling to get Sharky and Gnome to school and myself to work appointments, I have met up with a stranger on two wheels practically *every* morning for several years. The original Bicycle Guy routinely appears on the narrow, two-lane, no shouldered pike we drive. At one point Sharky and I became so frustrated, I considered penning an editorial for the local paper.

Look, I'm a fan of exercise. Not necessarily a participant, but still, a fan. I admire people who rise early to work out. But, I want this Bicycle Guy to get out of my way! I hate starting my day with a string of menacing moments and thoughts like, *Geez, I want to pass him but what if he turns? Geez, I guess all those cars behind me think I'm just slow. Geez, I wonder how much sweat is in those shorts.*

I never want Sharky or Gnome to be disrespectful toward grown-ups, but this guy wears us out. Once, when it was safe, I swerved quite dramatically around Bicycle Guy (so he'd notice) and nodded to Sharky, who then yelled out his backseat window, "Grab a napkin, 'cause you just got served!"

So, cyclists, if you are reading this, please understand and take this message to heart: The reason motorists yell, swerve, honk, and flip you The Bird comes down to two basic reasons.

1. You are making us late.
2. We are terrified we are going to hit you or cause a wreck by avoiding you. Not on purpose, of course! I mean, *I* won't lose mental control and just run you over.

Call me ignorant and do forgive me. I am just trying, like many drivers, to understand and—what's that weird bumper sticker I see all the time? *COEXIST*? Yes, let's safely coexist on the twisted roads of East Tennessee. Bicycle Guys, please stop being so selfish. Please consider the following observations, conjectures, and questions, and rethink your routines:

Like most mothers, I can never drive with two hands. When Gnome screams for a French fry, I must deliver. When Sharky smarts off, I must pinch. When Gnome drops his juice box, his book, his toy, or his blanket, I lean back and reach blindly (eyes on the road) and sweep the crumb-y gooey floorboard until I retrieve all of the above.

You are way too trusting toward strangers and their vehicles. My 2000 GMC Jimmy SUV, Big Red, is running on love and duct tape these days. My beloved Big Red is a menace to the work week as it is. She caught fire at a baseball tournament. Her driver's side door fell off in my work parking lot, twenty-five miles from home. My coworker got sick of customers telling us that someone left her car door open, so she crawled through the passenger side and jerry-rigged it shut. The door fell off again at a park, in the rain, when I was attempting to exercise. Typical. I had to hold the door onto the car until I got to the first—and naturally most expensive—repair shop I could find. My arm was sore for days. Last year, Big Red and I survived three winter months without wiper blades or heat. *Heat.*

In other words, Bicycle Guy, if my beloved Big Red treats me this way, how do you expect her to deal with an annoying two-wheeled insect humming in her periphery?

Drivers and their vehicles have issues beyond your control. We have bad brakes, bad alternators, loose belts, slick tires.... We could be arguing, reading, eating, drinking, napping....

Your outfits are distracting. My old fourth-grade teacher used to sing a song that went, "Keep your mind on your driving and your eyes on the wheel, because the girls are in the backseat with Fred." I can't keep my eyes on my driving when your muscles flex round and round in neon in my line of sight. Why *do* you wear neon in the daytime? Do you wear sunglasses at night? What's really bad is when your neon top doesn't match your neon bottom. I'm from Pigeon Forge, but still, come on! Also, what's up with the padded man Spanx? Are you trying to avoid chafing? Makes sense, but why not cover your man Spanx. Is this an aerodynamic goal? How much time can you really shave off with that get-up? If you bike to work, does that mean you walk into your office sporting man Spanx? You've already made countless people late for their jobs, and then you expose your colleagues to a middle-aged body bulging out of sweaty Speedo shorts first thing in the morning. If I saw that, I'd drop my donut!

Do you stink all day? If I rode a bicycle around my neighborhood, I'd become a one-woman rainforest. You *must* be physicians, because banks don't have showers and there is no way a teacher is going to take his clothes off at school. We hope. Is this how we get staph infections from minor surgeries, doctor?

Your bike weighs around 25 pounds. Big Red weighs 4,164 pounds. You do the math.

Why does your hat have a tail?

Why don't you ride on greenways and mountain trails? This is East Tennessee! Think of the views, the hills that could build those thighs and maximize your gluteus, the wildflowers.… Be men! Even I, Bug, the non-athlete with slow-twitch muscle fibers, stood up and pumped my maroon and silver bicycle all over The Crippled Beagle Farm, balancing her through rutted pit and tar roads dotted with box turtles and American Bullfrogs. I dodged sunbathing beagles and cow patties. I steered clear of barbed wire and electric fences to avoid Delicious's constant threat of tetanus shots. My skillful steering and command of the two-wheeled vehicle took me to shady spots where I would lie on a beach towel to enjoy *Sweet Valley High* books. I just don't understand why you have to absorb a whole lane on Lyon's View or Kingston Pike or Cumberland Avenue.

I'm curious; how do bicycle guys feel about motorcycle guys? And vice versa?

Speaking of Lyon's View, you know there's a country club on that road, right? I suggest you coast through its parking lot when you have extra time. You will see an inordinate number of white-trimmed blue squares framing stick men in wheel chairs. These handicap spots take up half the parking lot. Picture this: An elderly man arrives at the wood-paneled workout room at 6 a.m. to walk his twenty heart-healthy minutes on the country club treadmill. He then enjoys some cottage cheese and peaches with decaf coffee in the men only dining area. He gets in his giant Cadillac and pulls his cataract glasses from atop the visor. And, BAM! You meet. Bicycle Guy, you are placing a lot of faith in geriatric vision. Think about it. Lots of old people turn their whole torsos just to look left or right. And, they are always having eye treatments. Is that why you wear neon? Does neon glow in the cataract dark?

When you exit Lyon's View and head down Kingston Pike toward The University of Tennessee campus, do you realize you are in West High School territory? Does the term "Driver Education" mean anything to you? You are basically playing Frogger on wheels with high school freshmen. I taught freshmen. When a student told me, "Mrs. Bug, I'm getting my learner's permit today," I gulped and prayed. For all of us. Trust me, you are safer on the greenway.

Do you avoid the greenway to avoid other exercisers? Are there greenway hogs? Walkers, joggers, women behind baby strollers? Dog walkers managing unpredictable runaways?

Can't we all just **Coexist**? There must be some rules, some exercising etiquette. Ladies, make room for the cyclists, please, so I can get to work on time.

I told my dear old friend, Mutah, who is an active cyclist and often makes seventy-mile trips through the mountains, about this post and he told me that he and his friends have been "spit at, cussed out, passed way too closely, and even hit by cars!" He has a license plate that reminds people to share the road. He explained, "One bike rider was hit by a full sixteen-ounce Dr. Pepper bottle." Mutah warned, "I hope and pray your writing does not make you sound like one of these redneck idiots but instead tells people to share the road. The law states that they have to be three feet away from the cyclist."

I'm just going to have to say to all you bike riders, "Look twice for Big Red and thank God for her brush guard."

Bicycle Guys, I do admire your courage. I admire your tenacity. I admire your commitment to physical fitness. Actually, often, I admire your physiques, from a safe three-feet of distance, of course. Now and then, though, as I check out your toned thighs and well-defined calves, I get an up-close shock when I realize you are actually Bicycle *Girls*.

Owl Squad members age gracefully.

Theory 13: As people get old, they morph into the opposite sex.

Delicious loves to people watch, and often has me cruise her around Knoxville in Big Red, whip through Chick-fil-A for a sweet tea with extra ice and lemon or an Icedream Cone, and then park in front of Office Depot and Catherine's (a clothing store for plus-size women). We enjoy our treats and observe shoppers. We note trends in fashion and trends in form. We often notice how as men and women age, they morph into the opposite sex. Private parts don't change, but public parts become ambiguous.

Delicious had a student who said something profound once. He said, "As people age, they become caricatures of themselves."

Sharp noses point harder. Pendulous breasts drag south. Ears expand. Knees knot. Let's just work our way down the human body, shall we?

Hair

Back in 1996, I visited my college sweetheart at law school on his Ole Miss campus and, suspicious of his commitment to our long-distance relationship, searched his bathroom drawers. I found no lipstick, thankfully, but I did find Rogaine. Some men pamper every last strand with "product" and precise comb-over primping. There's a Bible verse: "But the very hairs of your head are all numbered." (Matthew 10:30) Why don't guys take this to heart and head? Some of you are predestined to be bald, right Presbyterians? Embrace it! Many gentlemen do accept their slick realties. My friend Happy Hour shaves what's left, dresses in dapper businessman fashion, and sports the look quite well. I saw a T-shirt once that read, "This is not a bald spot. It's a solar panel for a sex machine." Preach! Remember, boys, women fall in love with what they *hear*.

Ironically, as men cling to the last lock, women do the opposite. Grandmothers go for short, easy haircuts, and perm their hair up and out of the way. I'm only in my forties, but when my fabulous Blount County, Tennessee, Ross & Co hairdresser, The Stylist, looks over my shoulders into the salon mirror and asks, "What are we doing today?" I respond, "Cut my hair so I don't have to fix it."

The Stylist's salon was only five minutes from my office, so I made weird appointments with her at times like 4:10 and 5:05. Minutes. Convenience. Inches. Wet-cut-pay-hit the highway. You working mothers know the drill. I find it ironic that when I was a housewife for three glorious years, I used Great Clips to save money, but now that I'm working and have a little cash, I use The Stylist to save TIME.

Oh! Mini-Theory: People who have time *and* money should be on their knees thanking God. I once heard a predictably effeminate home designer on HGTV say, "Every night before I go to bed I pray that people with taste get money, and people with money get taste." Amen! Every night before we go to bed, millions of working mothers try to reconcile hours and dollars. Good thing The Stylist is efficient, affordable, and good at her work.

Delicious, who has sported a tight crop since the late '70s, counsels, "When women get real short hairdos they need to wear bright lipstick and big earrings so they don't look like men."

When I was about fourteen, I ruined Grandmama's hair. I used crochet hook to pull her curly-permed strands through a hole-punched swim cap and I lathered on store-bought peroxide. We tried toner, but to no avail. A Georgia fan all her life, she cringed at her singed Big Orange locks. She chopped it all off. Her recovery "do" was so short, my uncle asked her if she heated tweezers on the stove to use as a curling iron. My lovely Grandmama hid the tight mess under a baseball hat, which coordinated well with her favorite Dollywood T-shirt. One afternoon, driving in slow touron traffic on the Pigeon Forge Parkway, a man rolled down his car window and, in a sharp Ohio accent yelled to Grandmama, "Hey, buddy, can you tell me how to get to the Apple Barn?"

Grandmama dipped her chin and lowered her voice to a deep gruff to say, "Just go through the next light and take a right."

Her children and grandchildren gobbled up this funny story and nicknamed her "Buddy."

Faces

I know; broken capillaries cause rosy cheeks, but old men look like they are wearing blush, or, as Buddy called it, "rouge." In contrast, female faces turn pasty white. Delicious told me, "No matter how much time I spend slappin' on my war paint, I still look old when I finish." These days, I buy my makeup at the grocery store. Convenient cosmetics rule my beauty regimen, but as I lean toward 50, I know I'll need thicker, stronger coverage and color. There is hope! Merle Norman. Thankfully, my dear friend Micheelskin (named for her middle school obsession for eel skin wallets, handbags, and eyeglass cases), owns a Merle Norman shop in Foothills Mall in Maryville, Tennessee. And, she delivers. Women of Blount County, between The Stylist, Micheelskin, and the Smoky Mountains, we should be immersed in beauty. There is no excuse for us to look like men!

Mouths and Voices

Men's full lower lips plop into permanent pouts. Women's lips tighten and require plumpers, liners, and gloss. We are still expressive, but our once sexy chops turn to razor thin equal signs when we concentrate and wrinkled bulls-eye rooster butts when we fume. Smoker mouths are especially creased and shrunken. The male voice softens and pitches higher, like a "just over laryngitis" attempt to sound normal (I think some arterial blockage causes it). The female voice deepens. Visualize with me: A stooped mountain woman in sweatpants and flannel slowly dismounts from her pickup. She tosses her cigarette and enters the gas station. At the counter, she slaps *The Daily Times* on Formica and growls in Appalachian dialect, "Honey, gimmee a fill up and a five-dollar Jumbo Bucks."

As a former banker, I can assure you that this woman does *not* pay with a Visa debit card. She "don't trust 'em." I can also assure you that she has batteries, a generator, canned food, and bullets (paid for in cash so they aren't traceable by the gub'ment) stashed in her crawlspace.

Breasts

Bras are mini-prisons. When women age, they become more comfortable with the way they look. As our parts slide downward, our priorities shift upward. We become confident in who we are, stop obsessing over how we look, and seek comfort. We drop our workbags, groceries, cleaning, pocketbooks, and bras as soon as we hit the front door. My close friend, Elaine (that's her nickname, not her real name), no longer waits 'til she's home. After a few martinis at an Oscar watching party, she announced, "I can't take this anymore! These chicken cutlets are making me hot." She reached into her bosom, extracted two silicone bra inserts, and slapped them on the coffee table. Elaine is part of my close group of girlfriends. We call ourselves the Owl Squad. I can't remember why. Maybe because we are wise? Anyway, the Owl Squad has a Cheers — El Charro Mexican Restaurant. We are Facebook friends with the wait staff, the margaritas are, ahem, efficient, and we can be as loud as we like because we are regulars. El Charro is our comfort zone. Not long ago we all met there for supper. Elaine was last to come in, so

I asked, "I saw your car when I got here. What were you doing out there for so long?"

She casually replied, "Taking off my bra."

As women drop their bras, may I suggest that their newly well-endowed husbands pick them up and strap them on? I get self-conscious around man-boobs. Nipples are nipples. Duct tape some dimmers over those headlights. Or wear sports bras. If you don't want to wear dimmers or bras, could you at least wear some kind of squeezers? There is a reason the woman who patented Spanx is a zillionaire. For around fifty dollars, you can compress your way out of insecurity and into sexy self-confidence. I'm not sure you men could handle the temporary discomfort, however.

Waistlines

In college, I could feel my hipbones, but the glassblowers of nature and time have inflated my svelte form into a bumpy marshmallowy landscape. Delicious, who is quite cylindrical, swears she can wear her pants backward and no one can tell. She recently said, "Bug! I was at the grocery store and my shirt was drivin' me crazy! I couldn't figure out why it didn't feel right. Then I realized all the beaded parts were on my back. I had to go to the public restroom and twist the whole thing around." Thank goodness, she stopped wearing those shirts with necklaces sewn onto them.

As a bank branch manager, I had a perfect perch from which to observe the human form: from behind. My office looked out onto the customer side of the teller line. Here's what I noticed:

Women's round bottom parts shift up and out from the tailbone to settle like waist-high storage compartments like little hip seats for grandbabies! From the top, they shrink into coffee bean cracks. Actually, the whole body shape goes concave to convex. The forty-something's sport muffin tops. Call mine Otis and Spunkmeyer. The fifty-something's and above sport substantial panniculus (known in East Tennessee as feedbags). These panniculus (or should I say "panniculae" since I'm sure the word is derived from Latin, thus, toga fashion) may not be attractive to men, but they provide a soft place to perch in grandmamas' rocking chairs. Men's bodyweight shifts. Maybe nature orders, Sergeant Carter style, "Front and center!" Skinny shoulders. Bony legs. Even their hair migrates toward their midsections. Male rears disappear. Call 911! Somebody stole Tall Child's behind!

I guess that's why old men don suspenders and elastic waistband golf pants. No more zipper flies and sexy Levi's. Or, is the elastic meant to accommodate the cafeteria fetish? A perfect night for an old man in elastic: Meat and three at the early bird 4:30 p.m. special in buffet pants. It's a no-fly zone! Home in time to conquer Sudoku. A hot cup of decaf as he watches "The Wheel."

This makes me think of an old Sunday school song I loved as a child that I can now rewrite.

Deep and wide, deep and wide,
There's a [mountain mama] growing
deep and wide....

In general, with the exception of hair, women expand and men reduce. That's why I married a much taller Tall Child, so I'd have room to grow. From up there, I'll hopefully look small, even if I am wide.

Feet

As they age, women kick the heels and finally wear comfortable shoes. The damage is already done with varicose and spider veins, but who cares? They can run with the wind! — or try! Delicious spends big money on her comfortable sandals. They have just the right amount of leather to be cute but still cover her Band-Aids. Old men sport sandals, too. Sometimes with socks. Here's a tip from the Deep South. Men may be sockless only when wearing loafers. You are not Moses in the desert. You are Roger at Dollar General. Hairy toes are a no-no. My friend Deadline Diva, a talented writer and editor, eloquently said, "Toes look like freakin' little sausages wagging along." Toe*nails* are just plain gross. Paint them (ladies) or cover them up (ladies and men). Please! One of my sassy middle school students asked one day, "Mrs. D, when you gonna' let us see yo feet?" I know what she was up to. She wanted to identify a weakness, something she could use against me. I had a hairy-toed, Roman sandal-clod female teacher once. I made my first F in that class—on a quiz comparing Roman and Greek mythology. Athena or Minerva? Hermes or Mercury? Ugh. Who could concentrate? I had to focus my mental energy to avoid seeing her hairy toes.

Body Hair

Except for toes and cleavage, male stubble gets spotty. Their skin thins, revealing soft purpura-dappled forearms, calves, and ankles. They soften. Maybe it's menopause, maybe it's hormone replacement, maybe it's just tough life experiences manifesting physically, but women grow whiskers. The next time you see an elderly woman, get close enough to inspect her chin. She won't have a five o'clock shadow, but she'll have whiskers. This lovely new growth begins at middle age. I am on the constant lookout for rogue hairs on my body, which is why I'm armed with tweezers and a Bic razor everywhere I go. Especially in my beach bag. You see, one time, four hours into a 4th of July party at a fancy country club, I stretched in front of the mirror and thought, *Who are those little boys? They shouldn't be in the ladies' room. I do like their crew cuts, though. Oh, wait! Oh, no! Those are my underarms!*

"Older women make beautiful lovers." Furry ones don't. Are you prickly ladies expecting a knock from the Big Bad Wolf? If not, why do you look like you are dying to say, "Not by the hair of my chinny, chin, chin?" Ladies, face the music. You are morphing. You have whiskers. Lather up and shave!

Body Temperature

As the sexes age, they swap temperatures, too. Young women freeze. Menopausal and post-menopausal women roast. Young men roast. Old men freeze. I visited Delicious's old Corinth Baptist Church in Georgia. The sweet, Southern house of God ministers to one-hundred-some-odd congregants each Sunday morning. In many of the rows, dark blue and plaid throw blankets, meant for the men, lay across worn arms of aged pews.

The elderly Boss Hog constantly asked each of his beloved children and grandchildren, "Don't you need a sweater?" He hated to see us barefoot outside and was convinced we'd get pneumonia if we didn't wear shoes. As we planned a July beach trip, he said, "One night we should make a big pot of spaghetti!"

Dogwood Deb replied, "Yes, daddy, that's just what everyone wants after a long, hot day in the sand and sun. Spaghetti." Those beach condos have too many mirrors and glass top tables. I never want to see my reflection or thighs as I slurp noodles in a swimsuit.

Behavior

Now, these gender-morphing changes aren't only physical. Old men go to the mall, ostensibly to accompany their wives, but I see them jiggle and snooze in massage chairs while their wives shop. Women simplify. They carry the same handbag year-round and wear pretty much the same outfits and jewelry all the time, like uniforms — shopping outfit, babysitting outfit, church outfit, party outfit. I have every pair of earrings I have ever bought or been given — don't be too jealous; only one pair is real gold. My Claire's Boutique baubles fill a stack of ice cube trays in my bathroom drawer. I have options. But guess what. I wear the same $2.88 Walmart silver hoops all the time. With the same jeans and Target long-sleeve T-shirt. Boring? Yes. Liberating? Heck, yes!

Men gossip at barbershops and convenience stores. They become hypochondriacs and worry about family relationships and obsess over the weather. Women learn to say "No."

Women stop cooking. Men start grocery shopping. That takes some training. My dear old retired father-in-law heard Bop say, "I'm out of baking soda." Boss Hog jetted off to the grocery store and came back with a Cheerios-sized box of baking soda and bragged about his bargain-hunting conquest. Bop quipped, "Well, I'll never have to buy baking soda again. Ever."

Men get sappy, corny, and much less aggressive. Women speak their minds and take risks. No joke. Sharky, the Gnome, and I were parked and an elderly lady pulled out of the spot beside us and cut to turn, way too close to us. Instead of backing up, she slowed to three miles per hour and stared me down, as if to say, "I know you think I'm going to hit you, but watch me work magic, little girl." It. Took. Her. For. Ev. Er. Sharky had time to hop out, watch her for a bit, and hop back into the car! He swears her left headlight grazed Big Red's brush guard.

Women drive, and men ask to stop to go the bathroom. Women play golf and men go to Bible study.

And, most annoyingly, men start answering the house landline.

Somewhere off I-40, Bop (around age seventy-five at the time) stopped at Wendy's for lunch and a bathroom break. After washing her hands, Bop turned from the sink and came face to face with another patron. She took one look at her fellow customer and gasped, "Oops! I didn't realize I was in the MEN'S room!"

The person grunted, "I'm just as much of a woman as you are!"

In a noteworthy married couple argument, a rightfully mad Tall Child joked, "If you were a man, I'd hit you right now."

Well, Tall Child, it's just a matter of time before I am. By the way, when you start doing the grocery shopping, don't forget my shaving cream.

Delicious made this. She loves Christmas and Tall Child.

Theory 14: You can't make something into something it ain't.

Do you remember the old Chiffon margarine commercial, where Dena Dietrich tastes the margarine, thinking it's superb butter, only to find out she's been tricked? She swirls her chiffon gown and says, "It's not *nice* to fool Mother Nature!" If this is true, then why do people attempt to tame Mother Nature, odds, and physics? What are we trying to prove?

Outside cannot be inside. No matter how much money you spend. Hey, we all admire a perfectly executed outdoor wedding. But…

Imagine the scene: A majestic doorway opens; a crowd of adoring friends and relatives stand and turn in awe of an angel in white. Beautiful music pulls her through perfectly fabric-draped chairs in rose-adorned rows. A lovely breeze whispers softly through her perfectly curled tendrils. She used anti-humidity hair spray. She is unstoppable! She has fooled Mother Nature! She will *never* get divorced!

But, then…THUNDER! LIGHTNING! Rain. Humidity. It's your parade, bride, but the cliché promises rain on your parade. Why not take the parade safely inside?

Which backdrop is better: empty choir seats and a flat baptismal, or a field of wildflowers at sunset? I get it. But chignons become sticky bun Cracker-Barrel-gift shop-worthy puzzles of hair gel and bobby pins. Female guests look like dwarf stilt-walkers as they poke their way over grass lawns in their stilettos to and from the food line. Tents don't take wind as well as, say, I don't know…brick.

Many years ago, Delicious and I, with three hundred other folks, packed into an expensive rented tent to sweat our way through a friend's wedding. A groomsman passed out. I got windburns from Delicious's program folded into a fan. Afterward, we all went inside the adjacent country club ballroom to enjoy a roomy, air-conditioned reception. Why didn't we go there in the *first* place?

Nature always wins. For example, Tall Child took a large bottle of Round-Up weed killer to The Crippled Beagle Farm. He squirted his way down the gravel road fence row, thinking he could kill a quarter mile of brush with a chemical spray. A cousin spotted my city slicker husband and asked, laughing, "What does he think he's doing?"

I replied, "Tall Child is out killing trees with weed-out. After this, he'll probably Windex West Town Mall." I grade Tall Child an A for effort and an F for results. On his way back up the driveway, he passed an ugly thicket of privet and gave one last squirt. Delicious watched him holler and hoof it up the hill in a swatting frenzy. A farm-wandering, mean-spirited peacock had jumped out of that thicket and spooked Tall Child.

A few years later, a beloved and knowledgeable farm hand got the job done. All he had to do was pull the entire barbed wire fence out of the ground, bulldoze the tree-tangled line down, backhoe all the brush, and burn everything over a few weeks' time. I showed Tall Child the farm hand's success, and he said, "Well, I got things started for him when I sprayed that Round-Up."

"Luxury camping" or "glamping" is a trend nowadays. If you ask me, there is no such thing, *except* when my best buddy Downton Gams books a spot at Elkmont Campground. She brings every experience to the next level. She even wears a little bandana tied around her neck. With pearls, of course. Gams can sear a ribeye, roast asparagus, and host friends and children to see synchronous fireflies.

But, campers are still sleeping outside. I keep one eye open and wait for a black bear to rake his paw down my side of the tent. As good as Gams is, she can't control the temperature. Comfort is a constant goal that Delicious seeks—in wardrobe, travel style, and sleeping conditions. She *must* have air conditioning. Having said that, she's in no way a princess. As a matter of fact, she and my father chilled The Crippled Beagle Farm house with a window unit air conditioner and warmed the poorly-insulated old place with kerosene and space heaters. Because such heaters are dangerous, I had to shut my heater off at bedtime. I layered on a sweatshirt, sweatpants, flannel nightgown, and tube socks (Tall Child, if you are reading this, please calm down) to survive freezing nights in the holler. When I woke up, I could often scrape iced condensation from the grooves in my wood-paneled walls. Delicious is tough and does not complain, but she does enjoy creature comforts.

She, Pooh, and I tried to camp once. We hauled sheets, blankets, pillows, firewood, a cooler packed with their beer and my Cokes way up on a hill on our farm. We built a fire, enjoyed Lays potato chips, Mayfield onion dip, and family banter. However, we didn't sleep too well on our thin bedding, partly due to nature's stone-riddled mattress but mostly due to our beagles' excitement over having rack buddies on their turf. They licked and slobbered. They showed off. They took off, full speed, into the woods to bark unsuspecting rabbits into anxiety attacks. They rolled in cow patties on the return trip, and literally howled with delight and panted lord-knows-what bad breath all over our campsite.

Delicious declared, "Pioneer women and men roughed it and went through hell to learn all these lessons and create a better way to live. I will <u>never</u> camp again. Camping is flat out disrespectful to the pioneers."

I asked Delicious, "Why do you always say that camping is disrespectful to the pioneers?"

She explained in teacher tone, "Bug, they literally died by the droves on those covered wagons as they camped across America to settle the west. Imagine a yeast infection on the trail. I get enough *camping* during snow days when the power goes off and the well can't pump water."

One time, my grandfather looked over at a camper park <u>on</u> Panama City Beach in Florida, in July, and said to us, "Now that is absolute hell."

Not only do people try to make houses out of four-wheeled vehicles, they also try to turn motorcycles into cars. Remember, I grew up in a tourist town, so I scanned license plates my whole childhood. I still wonder why motorcyclists drive eight-plus hours through unpredictable weather, by choice. They wear rain suits and hang out under overpasses to avoid thunder, lightning, hail, and poor visibility. Ladies, think of all the stuff we absolutely need with us at all times. Where do you stash your handbag if you are a motorcycle mama? With those bulky, extra compartments and pieces belted to the front, back, and sides? By dragging those miniature trailers?

Delicious and I aren't high-rollers, but we do use hair rollers. We pack serious make-up bags. Clothes? We need options: Miracle Suits and generous cover-ups for day, colorful blouses and Capris pants for night, big pocketbooks, stretchy pajamas, etc. We proudly rep Faded Glory and Mossimo, and we have been collecting earrings since the eighties. My shiny stash has been passed over by a jewelry thief, however, it's important to me. As Delicious says, "You just never know what kind of earring mood you're going to be in." So, on all trips, we pack it all up and haul it all with us. Like many teachers, past and present, we're paranoid about lice, so we employ an arsenal of mousse, gel, and spray. Each morning, we spray a hair dome to protect ourselves and would not attempt to tempt fate on the road. How would that dome look after a day under a helmet in the Deep South?

Also, the best parts of road trips are talking all the way, hitting gas stations state by state for fountain drinks, using coins and the dashboard to scratch-off lottery tickets, and sharing boiled peanuts—none of which would be possible or safe on motorcycles. Plus, I don't want my rear-end any closer to asphalt than necessary. Plus, Sharky and the Gnome are typically in tow. Also, I can promise you this, as much as he loves me, Tall Child does not want me straddling him from the back, "log fluming it" with my mouth right at his ear from here to Hilton Head. And there *is no* way he'd let me drive. He can barely ride shotgun in Big Red without passing a non-existent kidney stone.

As children, my cousins and I set up fantastic "houses" in the cedar forest near the summit of The Crippled Beagle Farm. We outlined our floor plans with branch mazes. We upholstered sofas and beds with green moss. I even filled a recycled two-liter Coke bottle with water and wedged it between rocks over a hole to create a sink with running water in my "kitchen." That was playtime.

In the real world, bringing the outside in is inside-out thinking. I now live at the modest entrance to a nice neighborhood, affectionately tagged "The 9-1-9" (the last three digits of our tax-heavy zip code) by proud, over-mortgaged residents. Heck, I heard a fancy design shop even makes pillows and candles with "9-1-9" sewn/etched into them. Outdoor living rooms are all the rage in The 9-1-9. I guess, if you have enough money, you can play outside all year round.

Want to watch a bowl game on a chilly January night? Easy! Follow these simple steps.

1. Buy a rick of wood. One time, a bumpkin came to the door when I was home alone as a teenager, and mumbled, "I got here a rick a wood fer yer mama." I sent him away, sure he was there to rape me. When Delicious got home, I told her some man named Rick A. Wood stopped by. Mad as a wet hen, she informed me that he was supposed to deliver a rick *of* wood and she'd left a check on the counter. Oops! We *were* cold that night, but I *was* still a virgin.
2. Carry wood through your warm den outside to your patio and build a toasty fire.
3. Every thirty minutes put another log on the fire.

4. Keep the fire poker handy, and poke said fire, but don't let the children poke each other with the poker. Keep those toddlers out of the road. And the fire.
5. When the sun goes down, and the fire fades, turn on the fancy sideline/party standing heater you bought at Lowes.
6. Lay some dry blankets on the dew-dampened canvas furniture.
7. Warm the meatballs and wings in a crockpot.
8. Keep the other food warm by setting it on hot plates on the patio table. You'll probably need some extension cords. Don't let the toddler trip on the extension cord, while holding the fire poker, and land face first in the fireplace. It would really stink to have to go to Children's Hospital on a bowl game night after all this trouble.
9. Be sure to turn off the oven, lights, and living room television before everyone goes outside to watch the game.

While these open-air living rooms, decked out with Bose sound systems, Sony flat screens, Big Green Egg grills, Yeti coolers, and tongue-and-groove wood ceilings are fabulous, they are not a good money gamble in East Tennessee. Last Christmas Day it was seventy-five degrees outside and, a week later, seventeen. My Blount County bank customers would warn that money would be better spent on a basement stocked with survival gear. Perhaps. But, Americans are pioneers to our cores. We must tame the wilderness, one patio at a time. I'm no exception. My modest, covered patio sports a ghetto blaster, wood plank counter top, and ceiling fan. It's my favorite place to sip something cool and watch Sharky and Gnome shoot basketball. I have an outdoor kitchen, too, well, some might call it a fire pit. Upon close observation, some might call it a shallow hole Sharky and I dug in the backyard. Anyway, with the right amount of lighter fluid and newspaper, I can build a mean fire. I tried to cook hot dogs, but my coat-hanger camping fork was too short. I scorched my arm hair and burned my eyes, so I just walked down to the actual kitchen and, well, cooked them.

If you're going to make me eat outside, don't even try to force a veggie burger on me. My clever cousin Squirrelly Girly marvels at "Pretty much any processed foods targeted at vegetarians and vegans." She explained, "I take no issue with vegetarians' no-meat lifestyle, but I don't understand trying to fool themselves into feeling like they are eating meat when they are opposed to actually eating meat." I bet the same people who eat those veggie burgers also go to juice bars. My lovely buddy Fancy knows "someone" who got legally drunk at a juice bar. Hydrate before you healthy hydrate?

Teacher friend Honey Lips pointed out the endless struggle teachers face with oxymoronic "differentiated instruction assessed by standardized testing."

Sharky's seventh-grade girlfriend's mother, Sassy, Sr., remarked about how ridiculous it is for middle-school couples to say they are "going out." She and I agreed that Sharky and her baby, Sassy Sparkles, weren't *going* anywhere except school, school basketball games, and school dances. We parents have our methods. Before dances, the daddies take the boys out for Mexican food or pizza. The mama's take the girls out for sushi. Close dancing? Not for long. We also invoke the name of the Almighty as needed. Sharky went to a religious middle school, so chaperones were encouraged to spot any semblance of dirty dancing and remind those boys and girls to "make room for Jesus."

Sharky's very first girlfriend, Cheer Girl, kicked him to the curb about three weeks into the courtship, *after* I spent twenty-five bucks on Valentine's Day treats. You see, I took the romantic Sharky to Walgreens where he chose a box of M&M's, a funny card, and, after a half hour of deliberation, a stuffed pink elephant with a giant red bow between its ears. He was, however, nervous about the animal's serious Valentine message. The elephant held a heart-shaped pillow embroidered with the word "LOVE." He asked, "Mama, can you please sew that *LOVE* pillow off?"

"Sure I can. Why?"

He said, "It's just too early in our relationship."

True. Two weeks later Cheer Girl texted that she "wasn't *ready* for a relationship." You know, I'm pretty sure that she started the break up text conversation, but her mother, Cheer Mom, finished it. How do I know? Because Sharky initially responded to the break-up text, but I chimed in to make sure he saved face and handled things like a Southern gentleman. I wonder if her mother knows, as I do, that, during the last exchanges of the sentimental dialogue, my son was outside playing basketball and her daughter was watching *Frozen*. Seriously. The beginning was all *High School Musical* while the end was totally "State of the Union." The breakup went something like this:

Sharky: I'm bored
Wuts up
Hello?

Cheer Girl: We need 2 talk

Sharky: K

Cheer Girl: I don't think this is working out

Sharky: Huh?

Cheer Girl: I just don't think I'm ready for a relationship

Sharky: K
Why

Cheer Girl: IDK
Just think so

I step in. And, perhaps, so does Cheer Mom. Hmmm....

Sharky/Bug: Did I do something to offend you?

Cheer Mom: No, I just think we are too young to manage a romantic relationship and the demands of 7th grade academics, as well as our athletic commitments.

Sharky/Bug: I completely understand. I probably wasn't ready for a real relationship either. I want you to know that I respect you.

Cheer Mom: I feel the same way. I'm glad we can still be nice to each other at school.

Sharky/Bug: Absolutely. See you tomorrow!

It's always weird the first time you see your ex. I tried really hard to be cool when I saw Cheer Mom at a school ballgame a few days later, but my stomach was in knots.

I'll give Sharky kudos. He has good taste in women. Both of his former girlfriends are studious, polite, athletic, and close to their parents. But, Cheer Girl was right. Sharky was not ready for a relationship — not without a driver's license, a car, and a dollar to his then thirteen-year-old name. "Going out" in middle school is about as logical as the recycled toilet paper my friend Aunt Kat Kat saw somewhere.

Keep it real and keep it realistic. Can we all agree to follow the laws of nature, accept and enjoy progress, and avoid personal messes by dating in college and eating inside?

Except for fall Saturdays, of course.

"Come here, boy."

Theory 15: Tailgate etiquette is *not* an oxymoron.

I'd like to give a shout out to my buddy Mint Julep for prodding me to write about tailgates. Mint Julep and her husband actually treated Tall Child and me to a private plane ride to Tuscaloosa to watch Tennessee take on The Crimson Tide. I hate to fly, so I downed two Bloody Mary's on the twenty-minute drive to the airport and one more at takeoff. Seriously, when I board a plane, I don't sit until I've held eye contact with the pilot. I want to see "clear eyes, full heart" and a salt and pepper crew cut. I'm pretty sure my liquid courage fueled the engine, and my will to survive flew the plane. Once we landed safely, we had a blast touring campus and cheering on the Vols.

Tailgaters travel a spectrum from gentile civilized folks dining on linen-draped tables in The Grove at Ole Miss to sweltering, sweat and bourbon-soaked, foot-stomping, two-bits screaming fans in The Swamp at The University of Florida. As a Division I clarinet player, and dedicated alumna, I've witnessed a wide range of behavioral demonstrations—from Southern chivalry, when I lost my ticket at the Tennessee-Georgia game and a kind gentleman gave me his extra, to Northern aggression when, at the 1994 Citrus Bowl, a victorious Penn State band made fun of the UT Band as we all boarded buses to head home. Whatever. Let's see *them* perfectly execute a circle drill in cut time at half-time, half-drunk.

Jerks.

Tall Child and I built our own little Tennessee Tradition. We hosted season after season of super tailgates. I joined his family in Lot 9 and then we moved to G-10, a multi-level parking garage beside UT's Thompson-Boling arena. We gathered up more family and dozens of friends.

We all loved snagging the top corner spot over the G-10 garage entrance because we could cheer on UT fans and harass the opposing teams' fans as they drove in. Once, Delicious and Big Booty J, both Georgia graduates, helped organize a huge Tennessee vs. Georgia tailgate party. Delicious draped a giant GEORGIA flag over the railing above the garage entrance.

She was so proud. It was upside down. We never told her.

Alongside the upside-down flag, we UT fans dangled a stuffed UGA bulldog on a long rope over the entrance and tormented Georgia fans as they rolled through. I saw this idea when I was in Athens, Georgia, with the UT band. A couple of trumpet players sat on the sidewalk as we waited to enter the stadium. Every time a Georgia car cruised by in the molasses-slow traffic, the boys cast that stuffed bulldog under its wheels. We cracked up as Georgia fans of all ages fumed as they crushed their own mascot.

I guess anywhere from 50 to 100 people meandered through that UT vs. UGA tailgate. Dogwood Deb and I were six months pregnant with Balloon Girl and Sharky, respectively, so we can actually reminisce about that tailgate — because we were the only two people who can actually remember everything. As someone in my family used to say, "The only thing worse than being the only guy drinking is being the only guy *not* drinking." Apparently, I'm just as loud without vodka as I am with it. We were all so obnoxious then that a tailgater who lived in Tennessee but grew up in Massachusetts walked three humid miles back to my in-laws' house because he, like anyone from New England, couldn't take the Southeastern Conference heat.

I don't apologize for my Southeastern Conference spirit or spirits. I come from a long line of tailgaters. The SEC is in in my DNA. Delicious, BBJ, Pooh, Gravy, and others made annual pilgrimages to the Georgia-Auburn game. They held homemade posters to encourage and infuriate mixed fans along that same Athens road. Delicious's favorite signs of all time read, "Pat Dye dates Geraldine Ferraro" and "War Eagles have peckers on their faces."

Back in Knoxville, Tall Child, our entourage, and I migrated to the supreme tailgating spot — a flat paved rooftop on a one-story building. No cars in the way, thousands of tent-ready square feet, and panoramic views of Neyland Stadium and the Tennessee River promised huge crowds and awesome game days. To grab the coveted spot, Tall Child set his alarm for 4:00 a.m. He hustled out of bed, packed the car, and jetted to campus to start setting up around 5:00 a.m.

We even hired live bands for the big games. All football fans were welcomed; none were judged. But, even though tailgating gets rowdy, there are rules. Tailgate etiquette is not an oxymoron.

Tall Child's Rules for Tailgate <u>Hosts</u>

Never run out of beer or food. I'll add liquor to that list. Beer is tough to swallow in the morning, no matter how, as former UT Head Coach Phil Fulmer would say, "fired up and focused" you are. There's a simple solution to this problem: one-part vodka, two parts Zing Zang bloody Mary mix. Add three green olives, one leafy celery stalk, and one pickled okra. (Pairs well with sausage balls.)

Beat your guests to the tailgate spot. The head guy has to be the first one there. Being a loving wife and co-hostess, I prepped my tailgate hero's gear on Friday nights. That gear included a flat screen TV, zip ties, duct tape, cables, a converter box, tablecloths, tables, decorations, propane, charcoal, a rainbow of coolers, beer, liquor, ice, and Tupperware'd, Ziploc'd ingredients for on-location cooking. I lined it all up in our living room for early morning, last-in-first-out, worry free car-packing. All Tall Child had to do was load everything into the car, seize our spot, unload everything, and set it all up. I usually hitched a ride or got a cab three hours later. The "before" scene is sober and stressful. I liked to show up when the zip ties and Tall Child were tight.

Invite a lot of people. I can't think of a better place than a tailgate to make new friends, get a job, or fall in love. Once, a couple from our crew was so "in love" in the parking lot they got caught and tossed from *campus.* Not the game, not the tailgate — CAMPUS.

Bring a first aid kit. Sometimes, boy meets girl. And sometimes, boy meets pavement. The first aid kits should address allergic reactions, alcohol poisoning, dehydration, and burns. Once, our propane grill caught fire and threatened to torpedo through tailgates and under a car-squished parking lot. Our quick-thinking, younger friend Renaissance Man had one of those YouTube-worthy adrenaline rushes. He lifted a packed Igloo cooler and dumped it— cans, ice, dip, and all—onto the flaming grill, saving us all from tragedy and litigation.

Tall Child's Rules for Tailgate Guests

Respect the hosts and haulers. If the host offers to haul your stuff, drop it off per his instructions and be punctual. Any man willing to fight to lay claim to a tailgate spot at 5:00 a.m. for a 7:00 p.m. kickoff should not have to wait for anyone. If you drop off a cooler, make sure its contents are packed with ice and the cooler rolls. There is a definite correlation between hard-charging, senior citizen tailgaters and rotator cuff surgery stats at university hospitals.

Designate a driver. Run-ins with the police take away from the spirit of the party. If you do get arrested, do it *before* we take the pimento cheese out of the cooler. It really sucks to leave the party to drain ATMs for bail money. We have less to spend on popcorn and T-shirts, and we risk missing kickoff.

Share. If you have a big car and a parking pass, don't roll up solo! Offer rides. "For unto whomsoever much is given, of him shall be much required...." (Luke 12:48)

Bring a chair. If you don't bring one, don't take the last one. And, think twice before you sit on a cooler. If you do sit on a cooler, and *anyone* makes eye contact with you, GET UP!

Guide your guests. If you invite a female Northern friend to a Southern tailgate or vice versa, give her the dress code. Girls in the South dress up for football games. Staples include big earrings, feminine blouses and skirts or dresses, and high heels or cowboy boots. For night games, make sure you sparkle. Nothing is more beautiful than the delicate face of a Southern beauty set off by team-colored rhinestones under stadium lights. What is it about those stadium lights at night? Belles, if you travel outside the SEC, do a little research before you pack. Tall Child and I tailgated with Indiana friends at Notre Dame. I showed up in a skirt and they wore sweatshirts. I froze.
Speaking of clothes, Tennessee fans, pick a shade of orange and stick with it. If you aren't sure which shade is right, ask Coach Ray Mears to send you a sign from heaven. I met him when he gave a motivational speech to the UT band. He told us that he coined the cheerleaders' phrase, "Go Big Orange," and he pointed out the one and only Tennessee Orange (of the five shades he wore).
Girls, if you wear heels, bring flip flops, because heels, vodka, onion dip, and standing in scorching humidity from dawn 'til midnight makes pretty little feet sore and swollen. Plus, at some point in the evening, you'll hear "Dixieland Delight" and feel the urge to clog. You don't want to shuffle-step-ball-change barefoot on concrete littered with charcoal dust and bottle tops. That's just not ladylike. Also, take it from me; it's not cool to clog if you have to hold on to a chair, a person, or the tailgate tent post to stay upright for your butter churn. Some of us need to do our clogging earlier in the day. As for splits, those are always welcome. Our girlfriend,

Splits, could bust out a move on pavement, grass, even gravel, if the song, crowd, and spirit(s) so inspired.

Respect invisible boundaries. Don't push your table across the line. Space is a hot commodity, and you don't want to start a feud with the guys beside you. When it comes to tailgate neighbors, remember the old poem, "Good fences make good neighbors."

My fellow tailgater and former colleague, Hot for Teacher, so named because she has a flawless figure that motivates middle-school boys to finish all their worksheets, knows how to work the tailgate scene. Being young and hot scored her Jell-O shots, food, and sometimes a ticket. Little Buddy brought her into the tailgating group as a friend. Then they fell in love and became the youngest couple with no children. So, Tall Child Tennessee VolunTOLD them to set up on early mornings. The responsibility overwhelmed Hot for Teacher, so she revised her game plan. She charmed neighboring tailgaters. Pretty soon, they saved our spot while she and Little Buddy slept in.

Keep a sound food: friend ratio. A-Boo says, "Don't bring half a tray of pinwheels and nine friends." Worse, don't come empty-handed. Would you show up at a church potluck with nothing? As a hostess, I always felt responsible for guests having a good time. Unfortunately, I couldn't control how many people showed up. Once, a fellow tailgater drove up mid-day in a six-seat SUV by herself. She plopped into a chair and opened a combo meal. One. Combo. Meal. When she went to the bathroom, my buddy RokNVol and I sneakily peeked into her handbag. We found a Little Debbie Swiss Cake Roll. ***ONE***. Little. Debbie.

Now, I normally don't eat sweets while I drink, but, RokNVol and I were so annoyed that the girl invited work people, rode solo when she could have hauled five folks, and brought an individual meal, I broke my pattern. RokNVol and I ripped into that thin cellophane and swallowed one roll each. We hid the evidence and knowingly winked at each other every time we saw the girl reach into her pocketbook.

Don't expect the host to think of everything and accommodate your friends or coworkers, whom he has likely

never met. If you invite extra people, entertain them. Don't leave all the conversing up to your hosts. Be a mini-host! All are welcome. Help them feel that way.

Bring ice. If you are a slow roller who typically shows up two hours before game time "really tired" from the night before, don't call the host and ask if he needs more ice. Uncle Trout pointed out, "When is the last time you <u>ever</u> heard anyone say, '*We've got too much ice'?*" Bring it.

Guard your own gear. Don't ask anyone to watch your stuff while you go into the stadium. Stay with it or prepare to sacrifice it.

Use your brain. Keep in mind that the presence of children and bosses change the dynamics of any party. If you bring either, take care of them. Don't let children sit right in front of the big screen TV that other grownups bought and hauled. If you bring your children, bring your children food and drinks. Trust me. Diet Coke and orange juice serve a different purpose under the tent and they certainly don't belong in sippy cups. Ooh, and keep your young'uns out of the Jell-O. This ain't a cafeteria and most hosts don't pack stomach pumps. It's okay to roll up with a baby stroller, but make sure there's a twenty-pound bag of ice in its bottom basket.

Control and contain your child. Hot for Teacher recalled, "I will always remember you bringing a Pack 'n Play for Gnome to hang out in one year."

Her friend chimed in, "It was more like one of those old school play pens." Yes, ladies, and I'm saving that tough and tumbled contraption for my grandchildren. Someone should invent and market team-logo tailgate playpens. Dibs on the patent.

Leave your rule book at home. Non-smokers, preachers, helicopter parents, don't tell adults not to smoke, curse, yell, drink, or eat sausage balls. This is their domain. No moral authority allowed! Party at your own risk!

Be clean. Please use hand sanitizer before you hit the sandwich platter.

If in doubt, DIY. Don't ask anyone, "Do you have room in your cooler for this?" Most will say yes, even though you will likely get a reluctant "yes," because we are nice and want you to have a good time. However, it's better if you just bring your own cooler. Even Sharky packed his own tiny cooler of Gatorade, Doritos, and fruit snacks. Good boy.

Be prepared for anything. Tailgates are like campsites. You never know what you'll need, so think ahead and pack wisely. Little Buddy reminded me of one of our favorite memories. A friend, who is about twenty years younger than Tall Child, was three-sheets-to-the-wind after a long day of libations. Not only did he have a great time drinking and pulling for his team, but he also fell in love! He described the girl as "awesome." Little Buddy described her, um, differently. Our beer-goggled buddy brought his lady over to our tailgate area and dropped her at the edge of our center tent. Tall Child, drinking a cold beer and watching the big screen TV, reigned from a nearby chair. Our friend swayed over and landed hard in the adjacent bag chair. He then slapped Tall Child on the shoulder and leaned in to slur, "Hey, Tall Child, you got a condom?"

Tall Child said, "Buddy, I haven't used a condom since 1985."

According to All Vol tailgater Grover, our ready and willing lover boy let friends carve a pig into his canvas of back hair for Memphis in May Barbecue Fest.

And, he earned his nickname: Hairy Trojan.

If you eat by the pound, pay by the pound. Renaissance Man cooked gourmet breakfasts of pancakes, bacon, and sausage on his griddle for the early-bird setup. He also cooked huge extravagant low country boils and chili for the lunch and supper crowds. If you have such a kind chef in your crew, bring ingredients or give him cash.

Prolong the party with a pre-party. RJP lived directly behind UT's Cumberland Avenue, a congested ribbon of restaurants and bars, affectionately called The Strip. Little Buddy once stuck a real pig head on a stake and put it in the front yard of RJP's apartment for the UT vs. Arkansas Razorbacks game. As girls walked by it, they gasped in disgust, but guys usually said, "Hell, yeah!" Renaissance Man stayed up all night roasting the whole hog and almost got roommates Silverback and RJP evicted from their apartment for creating a barbecue pit in the front yard. The irate landlord came over the next morning. Silverback's response was, "Well, you said we could grill out."

Respect the scene but remember that stuff is just stuff. Memories live forever. Hosts (hostesses) actually go to a lot of trouble to organize the food tables. We spread tables with ironed tablecloths, use real plates, decorate with flowers, hang battery-operated chandeliers, and designate areas for drink mixing, salty snacks, and sweet treats. Please don't slap grimy purses, fuzzy coats, empty bottles, and trash on our pretty *Garden & Gun* September issue inspired tablescapes.

Then again, feel free to sacrifice material items for a good time and great memories.

I lost a couple of solid fold-out portable tailgate tables. Our dear Notre Dame ACC friend, known here as The Irish Guard, loved to join one Southern tailgate a year. A stout Northern boy, he could pretty much drink anyone under our tent under the table. Until he dove into said table and split it in two.

I lost a second table at the UT vs. Marshall homecoming game. I started the eventful day in an athletic-department issued T-shirt and poncho on the intramural fields. I was practicing with the UT Alumni Band, a.k.a., the Old Timer's Band. Tradition dictated that I start early. With my clarinet and vodka. During the early morning practice, rain pelted our ponchos. I didn't feel a thing. I was wrapped in nostalgia and fueled by Pride of the Southland and Smirnoff. Practice ended abruptly. Thunder, lightning, old people, metal, and water don't mix.

Tall Child had dropped me off at 7:00 a.m. and rushed to set up our tailgate, so I had no car and no choice. I fast-marched a diagonal from the west end of Volunteer Boulevard to the east end of Neyland Drive, which was over a mile. When possible, I flip-turned into long buildings to take cover and cover ground. During my soaked, solo march through campus, I spotted only two people as dumb and/or intoxicated as I was. At Circle Park, I found refuge in the Student Services Building Ladies Room and tried to clean myself up. I looked like a linebacker who'd over-applied eye black. I carefully took the stairs to the bottom, braced myself, and ventured back into what RJP calls the "Marshall Monsoon." At least I had warm food and friends waiting for me at the tailgate, right? No. Exhausted and drenched, I staggered onto the patio to see Tall Child, all the guys, and only one other girl: Splits. They were huddled under our tent. The table sat, exposed and pitiful, outside the tent. Its particle board top buckled and dipped, holding water. Underneath the table sat coolers, food, beer, and liquor. Thoroughbred tailgaters, you know as well as I that there's only one way to handle that situation: drink. Hard.

Some of us never made it into the stadium. But, smart, industrious, resourceful Renaissance Man did. Three times. Little Buddy told me that Renaissance Man drank an entire fifth of Jack Daniels in the Marshall Monsoon. He got kicked out of the stadium three times but had a pocketful of tickets, and just kept going back in. After the game, he called Tall Child and me to come pick him up, but we couldn't find him. He kept telling us he was in Humes Hall (the freshman girls' dorm), but we finally found him hiding in the boxwoods at Hodges library. We were relieved.

A blistered bird in the hand is worth two in the bush.

I don't know why he was hiding.

Know your place in tailgate sub-society. Cousin Fuzz, a dedicated Vol fan, reminded me to address a particular party phenomenon: the folks who stagger up to tailgates where they know no one. She calls them stray cats. Fuzz says, "Stray Cats, you are welcomed. It's cool for you to drop in but know your role. Stay on the perimeter. Make friends and mingle. Just like the young'uns, you should never sit front row at the big screen. And, whatever you do, don't touch another man's alcohol."

RJP reminded me of a sickening stray cat display, when what he called a "vagabond gypsy chick" poured beer on the pavement and then slurped it up trying to get us to give her money for exhibiting such talent. She probably did need cash. She also needed Pedialyte and a shower.

Speaking of talent, I'll add that you should recognize and respect the one person at every tailgate Banera Caliente deems The Common Denominator. The Common Denominator is the drunkest person at the party. Everyone else's level of intoxication can be marked by his/hers. For example, one might say, "Little Buddy was only two-thirds as drunk as Renaissance Man at that Marshall game."

Respect marriage vows. Singletons and married folks, tailgates get tricky sometimes. All kinds of things can go wrong in the heat of team rivalry. Don't offer to keep your friend's husband company if he's too drunk to go in the stadium. If she wants to watch the game, use his ticket. He'll be okay after a little nap on the sidewalk.

Help. When it's time to go into the stadium, some tailgates pack up. HELP. Don't just set down your drink, check your tickets, and walk off. If yours is a late-night, post-game tailgate, remember that your host may have been in that parking lot since as early as 5:00 a.m. HELP. Bag chairs, drag coolers, and haul stuff to the host's car.

Hide your own booze. Tall Child used to rent out space in my 34J bra cups to carry our friends' airplane bottles. I honestly think it was a source of pride for him. Cousin Fuzz's husband Six Shooter has what I can only call a colostomy bag. It lies flat against his underbelly while a tube is threaded through his shirt to draw bourbon from tummy to tongue. Grover's brother, Pattywagon, bought some flip flops that had a flask in the heel for when UT played UCLA in the Rose Bowl. He filled them up with Jack Daniels at the tailgate, but after he walked around with them so long, the flask compartment popped. He squished around the rest of the day, reeking of whiskey.

From Sharky: No fighting. We'll see how long his rule lasts when he's a passionate college student. It's just so hard to control yourself in overtime. Even a docile band geek can infuriate you. RJP says, "I think Little Buddy throwing a cupcake at Alabama's tuba section is about the funniest thing I've seen. And the Bama band deserved it. They were at <u>our</u> tailgate spot playing the Bama fight song. What did they expect?"

RJP also appreciates diplomacy. After a loss to South Carolina, a rude Gamecock fan smarted off to us. RJP gave him three choices:

guzzle PGA punch with him, get his [behind] beaten, or leave. RJP said, "To the Gamecock's credit, he chose PGA."

If you do lose your Southern Comfort cool and attack a nearby tailgater by force, take a lesson from my cousin Roscoe's Division I performance: go for broke. Then go home. You see, once upon a tailgate time, innocent little Sharky was throwing football with a friend. He missed his catch and the football landed in a nearby tailgate. Some jerk picked up the ball and sailed it way out into the massive, crowded parking lot. Sharky was sad. Tenderhearted Roscoe loves Sharky. Roscoe strolled over, picked the guy up and dragged the guy down his own tailgate table like a bar towel, dropped him onto the concrete along with the table's food and beverage wreckage, and calmly disappeared into the sunset behind the port-o-potties.

A few years ago, a rich donor gave money to the UT School of Engineering to construct a giant educational building. The university dynamited our dynamite tailgate spot to construct the multi-story facility. I cried. Tall Child used the demolition and a losing season to hang up our tailgating cleats. I am forever thankful to every person who ever shared our tailgates—no matter how he or she behaved. Thank you for creating some of the best Saturdays of my life. Now that Tall Child has retired as Tailgating Torchbearer, he wishes all tailgaters great success as you cheer on your teams. Don't feel compelled to carry on our traditions. Create your own. But, *whatever* you do, *do not* break the number one rule in tailgate etiquette. **BRING YOUR OWN BEER!**

At least the basement looks better now.

Theory 16: Think you can do somebody else's job? Wrong, chicken lips!

I bumped down interstates for four seasons of college football with The University of Tennessee Pride of the Southland Band. Every time, and I mean *every* time we passed pastures of grazing cows, prolific along I-40 and I-75, this goofy brass player would say, "Why, those cows are *outstanding* in their field."

Think about it. Have you ever met a cow who performed poorly as a cow? Like I said earlier, healthy animals don't trip. How could a lion eat if every time he pounced on prey, he stumbled and gave himself away? Unlike the aforementioned tailgate stray cats, *real* cats know their jobs. Do you think a dog watches the neighbor's cat claw its way to the top of an oak tree and thinks, "That cat climbs at the wrong angle. Can she even get down from that height?" By the way, there is absolutely no need to rescue a cat from a tree. Humans panic. Does the cat watch the dog and think, "He's an idiot? Who buries a bone that deep in the dirt? He'll never find it."

We the People, on the other hand, do make mistakes. Unfortunately, we also criticize other people as they perform. All jobs require specific training, yet we think we understand and can assess the work of fellow humans. I did a little research in my friend and family field.

Do you relate?

Are you guilty?

SERVERS

Always tip twenty percent. I wrote "Theory 9: Everyone should work in a restaurant" for good reason. As a server I was criticized, talked down to, rushed, and stiffed. Little did my customers know that I had complete control over their breakfasts, lunches, and suppers. And heaven forbid a slow cooking line made them late for their Days Inn 11:00 a.m. checkout or the 7:00 p.m. Smoky Mountain Jubilee. Think of the potential consequences: A diabetic, who also happens to be hateful, rudely orders Diet Coke. An offended waitress brings her a "Diet Coke" alright, with thirty grams of sugar. A tightwad (there's nothing worse than a tightwad) leaves the server pocket change after running him to death. The next week, the tightwad signs his son up for tee ball. Guess who the coach is. Guess who rides the bench.

Tall Child's family LOVES to tell this story. To the congregation's delight, it was once even part of our former pastor The Confederate's sermon. Here's what happened. My dear old father-in-law was nicknamed "Boss Hog" by Tall Child's Hiawassee College basketball teammates because of his dapper style and circular shape. I adored my father-in-law. Unlike the misdealing Jefferson Davis Hog TV character, our Boss Hog's character was impeccable. He was smart, kind, affectionate, honest, generous, and honorable. He had perhaps only one major flaw: impatience. And, as a retired bank executive, he'd always had the luxury of a secretary. Boss Hog didn't take orders. He gave them.

Our beloved patriarch took the family on a beach trip to Wild Dunes in South Carolina. Boss Hog loved to go out to eat, so one night during our trip we all went to a waterside restaurant for some fresh seafood. Boss Hog sat, where he belonged, at the head of the large table. A cute college-aged waiter welcomed us, "How are you all doing tonight?"

Boss Hog said, "Doing well, and, how are you? We can order now."

Bop gently chimed in, "Daddy, hold on. We haven't even had time to read the menu."

The waiter took Bop's cue, and suggested, "Why don't I get your drinks first?"

Boss Hog said, "That will be fine, but when you get back, be ready to take our orders."

When the waiter returned, he stood beside Boss Hog, ready to do his work. Boss Hog didn't give the guy a chance. He took control and said, "Okay, we'll go around the table and each of us will tell you what we want to eat." Like a wild conductor directing cymbals to clash, Boss Hog pointed to Bop and directed, "Tell him what you want." Now, Bop is *never* in a hurry, so, of course, to Boss Hog's utter annoyance, she asked a couple of questions about menu items and then asked to be skipped. That got Boss Hog all out of whack.

Boss Hog shrugged, "Fine. J-Bird, order." J-Bird ordered. Then Boss Hog pointed to family members, one by one, demanding, "Order. Order. Order." Ever her mother's daughter, at her turn, Dogwood Deb debated between shrimp and scallops, and asked the waiter his opinion. Frustrated at Dogwood Deb's inefficiency, Boss Hog said, "Deb, this man has a job to do."

It was at that epic moment that the waiter, still standing beside Boss Hog, confidently slapped his hand on Boss Hog's shoulder, and said, "Sir, why don't you clock out? I'll take it from here."

My commanding father-in-law picked up what the guy was laying down, and, true to his soulful humble nature, laughed at himself.

You know how certain phrases from memorable moments stick? I can't count how many times after that we told Boss Hog to "Clock out."

SALESMEN

Tall Child is a commercial sales rep for a local flooring company. He loves his job and his employers. After a year there, he told me, "I've found my calling."

I asked, "Carpet and tile?"

He added, "And hardwood."

Among his many professional gifts, Tall Child expertly communicates and is equally comfortable with customers, installers, sub-contractors, and CEOs. Just ask him about laminate vs. pre-finished, fleck vs. Berber. Don't even get me started on his knowledge of nylon fibers. The builders rely on his expertise, but, he insists, "Retail customers in the showroom think they know more about product and installation than I do just because they watch HGTV."

HAIRDRESSERS

I met my friend The Stylist when her son and Sharky played baseball together for the Knox Sox. She recently graduated from Tennessee School of Beauty. That's right, graduated from a specialty trade school, and said, "I have so many people in my chair tell me to give them five minutes and they could learn to cut hair. I want to tell them to go ahead and take my expensive shears. Go home and Google away. See if you can learn in five minutes what I learned in months of training."

Well, I tried. Once I began writing full time, I didn't want to drive 45 minutes to get a haircut. My styling skills and social life don't merit the time or financial investment. DIY-ing is my jam, so I watched a wikiHow TWICE (always an overachiever). I dipped my hair under the shower nozzle then wrapped a towel around my shoulders. I followed the wikiHow instructions and did an okay job. I thought. At Zumba class a few days later, I asked my bud Saint Rita to be honest. She said, "That's not your best haircut. I wouldn't go back to that salon." Maybe it was my Dollar Tree scissors. You need good gear. She urged me to see her guy. I did. Much better. Want to know something sweet? When it was time to pay, he said,

"You are taken care of." Thank you for saving me, Saint Rita! I promise to use hair products in your honor.

COACHES, REFEREES, ATHLETES

My Uncle Trout, who played basketball and baseball for Auburn University and coached high school basketball and baseball, once noted, "You know, when I look up into the stands at a ballgame and see parents who are doctors and lawyers, I don't think I can do their jobs. But, for some reason, they all think they can coach."

I think it's funny when Bop comes to Sharky's games and asks, "Why is that coach yelling?" One of Sharky's coaches, Rip City Knox, is so wild, and sometimes so controversial, that <u>grandparents</u> from *opposing* teams scold him post-game. He yells, squats, and swings his arms with masculine passion. On one knee, he slides on the floor from one end of the bench to the other. He probably holds the league record for technical fouls. But, I LOVE him. So does Sharky. Not only is he entertaining, he's a freaking awesome coach. And an exceptional father. He's a teacher with a temper, but only because he cares deeply for his players. Rip City Knox stills cheers Sharky on from the stands. In a seventh-grade semi-final tournament game, a player knocked Sharky, hard, out of bounds. Rip City yelled at the ref, "How did you not *see* that?"

The ref, familiar with Rip City Knox, cut to the inevitable chase. He looked at Rip City Knox, pointed to the door, and yelled, "You're out of here."

Once, he even made it to YouTube when a ref ejected him from the gym. Rip City Knox deliberately spent several minutes saying goodbye to his players, talking to his brother/assistant coach and packing his duffel bag. Fans gaped. Finally, he strolled across center court and took an elegant bow as opposing team fans booed.

Delicious and BBJ are the dynamic duo when it comes to coaching from the bleachers. No one is safe — especially the refs.

When my cousins played middle school ball, BBJ harassed the regular ref, whose first name was Dauber. Yep. Anyway, any time he made what she thought was a bad call, BBJ chanted, "Dirt dauber, dirt dauber, dirt dauber." For you city folks, a dirt dauber is a species of wasp that builds mud tunnels in your windows and doors.

Even female refs were targets. Sevier County had one particularly pathetic, thick-headed lady ref. Every time she missed a call, BBJ and Mooch yelled, "Get back to yer' iron'n board!"

Speaking of ladies.... You've surely heard of the Rebel Yell. Well, in equal parts boldness and weakness, I created a Butch Yankee Yell to disguise my voice. I mean, in the heat of Sharky's games, I sometimes lose it. With my wit and lack of self-control, I could really embarrass Sharky's team. Or worse, cause a technical foul. So, when Sharky gets a bad call, and I feel the urge to really yell, I lean low behind a friend, drop my chin and voice, and employ my best male Michigander accent to shout, "Oh, come on!"

I used to scream, "You have to make that!" when Sharky missed a layup. Until my friend Cougar Tutor, who has a boot camp fitness class every Saturday at my church, had us do a basketball drill. He perched a basketball on a cone under the goal and told us to sprint from the half-court line to the ball, pick it up, shoot it until we made it, then sprint back to half court. I think I took 24 shots, with no one guarding me, and made three. That was humbling.

"Hustle" was my other favorite word to yell. I couldn't understand why Sharky couldn't rebound, dribble, pass, and then bolt to the other goal. Until I had to do it. As I explained earlier, students find sick pleasure in humiliating their teachers. I was drafted to play in a faculty game. I wore a LeBron James Miami Heat jersey, knee socks, and ponytails, but I could *not* "hustle." I could barely run. And, when I did, I crossed my arms over my chest for fear my students would conjure up their own "Boom chugga lugga lugga" chant.

Delicious yells "hustle," too, and whispers to me, "You need to tell Sharky to stop loafing down the court." After each game, she needs two adults to help her down the bleachers.

How about you, gentle reader? Have you truly read and committed to memory all the rules of youth/college/professional baseball/basketball/football/golf? Are you in shape?

TECHNICAL EXPERTS

My friend Squirrelly Girly is a mainframe computer programmer working on billing systems, and she once had the *treasurer* of her company call her to tell *her* how to code a program. His favorite thing to tell programmers was, "It's just an IF statement!" He said that so much that it became an inside joke in the IT department. For those of us in the non-digital galaxy, an "IF statement" is a programming conditional statement that performs a function and displays data.

Oh, yeah, I use those all the time at work and home. Don't you? As in "IF I write a check that my @$$ can't cover, I will incur a $36 overdraft fee, which will be displayed on my bank statement and face."

Have any of you ever tried to write a macro in Excel? I tried. And tried. And tried again. Here's a What IF Analysis for you: What IF we start a company and put Tall Child in charge of maintenance, me in charge of employee fitness, and Delicious in charge of budgeting. As IF!

BANKERS

Bankers endure countless hours of annual regulatory education and testing to ensure they make sound loans, don't discriminate, and manage risk. I knew my job, but customers challenged me all the time. One said I should fire my assistant manager, Adele. I call her Adele because one day she had an instant message conversation with our friend Indeed. He's handsome, and he says, "indeed" a lot. Weary of the back and forth typing, Indeed messaged, "I'm calling you."

Adele's phone rang. She picked it up, and brashly bellowed lyrics "Hello from the other siiiiiiiiiiii hiiiiiiiiiiiiiiiiiiiiiiii hiiiiiiiidddddddeeeee." Unfortunately, Indeed was interrupted before he placed the call, so Adele actually sang to a customer who freaked out and hung up.

You have to love someone who sings at the top of her lungs even though she can't carry a tune. She exceeds her sales goals and takes great care to help clients. She "throws her soul through every open door."

So, back to the story. One day this bipolar (not a judgment—she told us) elderly client, obviously disappointed in her third husband, whom she married for his Social Security direct deposit (not a judgment either — she told us this, too) was as mad as a wet hen at Adele. The problem? The customer couldn't figure out how to activate her check card in the ATM. Adele calmly explained the process, "You put your card in, enter your PIN, and push the 'check balance' button."

The lady said, "You are being a rude smartass! I know it's more complicated than that! How dare you talk to me that way?"

She stomped over to my office and demanded, "You need to fire that bitch! I want her to come out from behind that teller window so I can slap her in the face. She is deranged!"

I'd overheard the whole conversation. I said, "Mrs. X, Adele is 100 percent correct. She's trying to help you."

Mrs. X said, "Make her come out here."

"No, ma'am. She is a good employee. I am not going to let you talk to her this way, much less hit her in the face. And, I will NOT fire her."

Mrs. X screamed, "WELL, THEN, YOU ARE DERANGED, TOO!"

An old man once carped, "I been banking longer 'an you been alive, and you ain't calca-latin' that interest right."

To which I carped back, "Well, sir, I've been eating food for forty-plus years, but I'm not telling the twenty-nine-year-old chef at the world-famous Relias & Chateaux Blackberry Farm how to roast the perfect turducken."

I nicknamed my dutiful, selfless friend Lifestar after the local hospital rescue helicopter. She's extremely overprotective, if not tenacious, when it comes to the well-being of her child, and, as a valued employee of Knoxville Utilities Board, Lifestar is responsible for repairing power outages in our community. She adores her child to a fault. She serves others tirelessly. She also loves to shop. Let me say that one more time. She *loves* to shop. Determined to find me a swimsuit top that actually fit and carried my load, Lifestar took me to the mall. We stopped in the fancy Ann Taylor shop on our way to my usual discount spots. I asked, "Lifestar, you come here all the time, don't you?"

She said, "Absolutely not. I don't know why you think that."

That precise moment, a clerk walked toward us and said,

"Hey Lifestar! We haven't seen you since Tuesday!"

While Lifestar is usually solid in a crisis, she didn't handle a debit card snafu too well. Her generous Christmas plans came under attack, and so did I, her banker. December 15, she texted me, "I need your help! My check card was declined. It's Christmas time! This is a nightmare!"

Her rotor blades whipped wildly. Off retail course and out of cash kilter, Lifestar needed saving. I investigated the issue and ordered Lifestar a brand-new card, which would arrive in five to seven days. I explained. She exclaimed, "How can I do Christmas without my check card? This is tragic, Bug. Do stores still even take checks?"

I said, "Stores take checks and cash. You will be all right."

Every day, she texted, "Card not here yet. Freaking out. Help! Do something!"

I texted, "I can't mold plastic and insert chips here at my East Tennessee branch. Hang and hover. You'll get the card in a few days."

The fifth day, she texted, "I am going to switch banks. Give me the name of the man in charge of debit cards. I can't survive Christmas without my check card! Heads are going to roll."

I said, "I *can't wait* until my power goes out the next time it storms in The 9-1-9. I'm going to text you every three hours until the lights come on. Heads are going to roll."

She said, "That's a little different. KUB always fixes things."

I said, "Sure, eventually. Once hypothermia sets in and I miss 'The Walking Dead.'"

She said, "KUB is not *that* bad."

I said, "No, you aren't. You are better than Comcast. Comcast sucks."

She said, "Well, your bank sucks right now because I don't have a debit card."

I said, "I thought of a perfect advertising slogan for KUB. You could give away bumper stickers that read, 'KUB: Better than Comcast.'"

Retail bankers are always on edge. They stomach unyielding loan underwriters, intrusive government regulations, long hours, and, sometimes, profanity and physical threats. It's sad to say that some people get more emotional about their money than they do their children. Anxious customers park in front of the door and wait for us to open. When I was a teacher, I had to beg certain parents to come to school for parent teacher conferences. FYI: Being handicapped or impaired does not give you the right to be a jerk. Neither does being dumb. Or insane. Or elderly. Delicious says, "Age is no excuse for rudeness."

Understand that the bank is a bank. It's not a social spot for you to hang out between your Hardees breakfast and your ten o'clock bridge game. It's not a copy shop. Don't get mad when we say we can't do something, like mediate your divorce or publish your book. Seriously.

A guy brought me a spiral bound college-ruled notebook filled with his "manuscript." He said, "I want you to publish this."

I said, "We don't publish books."

He said, "Why not?"

I said, "Because we are a bank."

He explained how important his work was and asked me to read it. I was tempted once I saw the title, written in magic marker on a homemade cover he'd Elmer's glued to the notebook:

Woman. Created by God, Destroyed by Man. He had a point.

I made copies of documents for two deaf ladies who visited my branch. They were not customers, but I didn't mind. Well, they returned every day for a week wanting more and more copies. I minded. I told them we'd have to charge them. They cussed me out. In American Sign Language. They cussed me so hard and so long, they probably got carpel tunnel syndrome. That was completely unfair. I only knew one hand sign. I was pretty sure it's not part of American Sign Language. I was also sure it would get me fired.

Not long after that incident, a guy with a tracheotomy blistered me because I wouldn't approve a check he wanted to cash. The funds were not available, but I was. For a whisper-growl tongue-lashing. He put that little microphone to his tracheal opening and went on a rampage. What could I do?

My favorite "almost fight" happened at the drive-through, which opened 30 minutes before the lobby. A scowling middle-aged woman idled in the lane. Tellers called me over. I flipped the switch on the microphone, and said, "Good morning. I'm the branch manager. How can I help you?"

She said, "I want to cash this check, and your teller said she can't find my account in your computer." I tapped her information into our software. No name. No account. No trace of her. I reiterated what my teller told the woman. She fumed, "This is ridiculous. You are doing this on purpose! Let me in the building."

I said, "Ma'am, I'm not sure how I can help you. Why do you want to come inside?"

She yelled, "I am coming inside to give you a piece of my mind!"

These days I show my temper only at home, but at that time I was in my early twenties and hadn't mastered self-control. I smarted off, "The bank lobby doesn't open until nine."

That overcooked her grits. She slung her car door open, jumped at the drive-through window, and put her finger on the glass. She said, "You let me in now. I am going to kick your ass!"

Safe and cocky behind bullet resistant glass, I stated, "No. I am not letting you inside."

She screamed, "Why the hell not?"

I said, "Because you are going to kick my ass."

"I'll wait 30 minutes. Then, I'm coming in."

A few weeks earlier, I'd gotten into the wrong car at the grocery store. I cranked and cranked but the car wouldn't start. My key felt funny in the ignition. I was about to let loose with foul language when I noticed foreign personal items in the passenger seat. I was in someone else's car. It hit me. I asked the lady, "Ma'am, what is the name of your bank?"

She said, "First Tennessee!"

I said, "You are at First American."

Instead of kicking my ass, she left.

Sometimes customers simply misinterpret our meaning, or, with my employees, our dialect. My last office sat only twenty minutes from one entrance to Great Smoky Mountains National Park. The community draws tourists and retirees, many of whom flee brisk Ohio winters to settle in a warmer landscape. They embrace our mountains but don't always understand our ways. For example, one furious Yankee customer bounced a few checks and racked up overdraft fees. Confused and upset, but in a Yankee-style hurry, she pulled into the drive-through to seek restoration from one of the tellers. The East-Tennessee born and bred employee who dealt with the lady is salt of the earth and met her with a smile. The enraged check-bouncing Yankee snapped through the drive-through window microphone, "I do NOT understand why my account is overdrawn! You had better explain."

The teller did, saying, "Well, honey, you done writ the far outa yer checkbook."

STORE CLERKS

As I child I was desperate to scan groceries. I watched this lady with long, curly, weird fingernails at the Sevierville, Tennessee, Kmart man-handle a ten-key every week when Delicious paid on her layaway. Finally, self-checkout lanes came about and I got to test my secret longing. But I choked when scanning produce. I routinely picked up produce with no bar code stickers and wasted precious time searching the scanner software for bananas. I got the urge out of my system. Now I rely on professionals.

At the old Proffitt's Department Store, Delicious would get so mad if no one was there to help her shop. You know how, when a store employee asks, "May I help you?" most of us say, "No thank you, I'm just looking" because we want a little privacy to berate our fat thighs and expanding panniculae? Well, not Delicious. When a clerk asks, "May I help you?" Delicious says, "You sure can!"

When I was growing up, she'd add something like, "Well, this is my daughter. She has a new boyfriend, and they are going to a dance, and we want her to look beautiful!" It was awful. She'd always work in the fact that I was in the band, too. Loud and proud. And annoying, because I hate to shop for clothes. Now she says things like, "Bug's a little worried about her tummy," or, "Can you help us find something slenderizing?" She loves to say "slenderizing."

If a tired Delicious, typically frustrated by my reluctant, sullen store behavior, couldn't find a clerk, she'd yell, "Help! Customer needs help!" until one arrived. Also, if an abandoned cash register desk phone rang for too long, she'd answer it, "Proffitt's Department Store, may I help you?" Then I'd hear, "No one is here. If I were you I'd give up and call Dillard's."

CONTRACTORS

Tall Child once thought he was a lumberjack. He said he wanted to chop down a tree in our back yard. It was at least 100 feet tall. I said, "Don't you dare try to do that."

A couple of weeks later, Sharky and I returned from a visit to The Crippled Beagle Farm to see one of Lifestar's Knoxville Utilities Board trucks, a Knox County fire truck, and neighbors gathered at some kind of spectacle in our yard. Tall Child had ignored my threat. As he and our neighbor cut a notch into the wrong side of the huge Tulip Poplar, it leaned precariously toward the road and a beautiful white house. The home's occupants panicked and called 911 and KUB. KUB's trained tree experts saved the road, the power lines, the house across the street, and Tall Child's behind. Did I mention this all happened the Saturday morning of the Tennessee vs. Florida football game and that, had the tree fallen, fifty-five houses would have lost power?

Home Depot plus the internet are an awesome combo. Those stores have helped women feel less helpless and more confident that we alone can take care of business. No more nagging and waiting, ladies. Google it, buy it, and follow the instructions. *You'll* show *him*! I've accomplished light electrical work, minor plumbing, and lots of painting. I can cut in like a pro. But, I've learned the hard way when to call in professionals.

My biggest project was painting the basement ceiling. Tall Child's head hit the ugly, commercial drop tiles in the 700-square-foot subterranean room of our basement rancher. So, I ripped out all the ceiling tiles, fluorescent lights, and metalwork. Raise the roof! Bad move. I figured I'd sweep out the dust and enjoy rustic, wood-clad headspace. Wrong. I forgot about pipes and wires. I exposed a big mess. First, I tried to get on HGTV show "DIY to the Rescue."

My essay compelled the production crew to come take a look. I got rejected. They said my project was "too large in scope for a three-day timeline."

My solution was to paint the basement ceiling bright white. I Googled, calculated, and took off to the hardware store to rent a paint sprayer. The only woman in the check-out line, I felt a bit judged. A flannelled man reeking of gasoline asked me, "Honey, you sure you can handle that thing?"

I nervously admitted, using one of Trout's famous lines, "Sir, I'm about to run mule in the Kentucky Derby."

Determined to save ceiling face, I hauled the eighty-pound sprayer and five gallons of white paint home. Just getting the machine in the house and down the stairs was an aerobic cuss-fest. I'm not sure if I ran the machine or it ran me, but we gyrated all over that square den until I'd used every drop of paint. I had miscalculated. I ran out of paint. I hustled back to Lowe's for more, looking like a transvestite Geisha coated in primer.

JOURNALISTS

Like all grammarians and English teachers, Delicious notices every flaw in another's speech. Luckily, she *only* corrects me in private. Oops. I mean to say, "She corrects me *only* in private." Sorry, Mama. TV broadcasters be warned. Delicious will call your boss. She phoned ESPN headquarters in New York City when a football commentator repeatedly mispronounced Auburn's "Jordan-Hare Stadium." Folks, it's pronounced "*jur*-den," not "*jor*-dan." Among others, she's called Lamar Advertising, a billboard company, *The Mountain Press* newspaper in Sevierville, NewsTalk 98.7, and Walmart.

For the love of God and all humanity, retail shops, please change your signs from "20 Items or Less" to "20 Items or <u>Fewer</u>."

LEGAL EAGLES

I refuse to jump on the trite lawyer-bashing bandwagon. Lawyers land on a spectrum from good to bad, just like anyone else. I know truly talented attorneys and judges, like my friend Little Linda. She is a practical, fair, realistic mother and wife. She "gets it." She's concise, too. Some basketball team mothers and I took our boys to the Tennessee Valley Fair one hot September afternoon. Little Linda found essential action to execute in her three-hour tour through carnival games, rides, and concessions. She paid $1 to view the fair's freakiest exhibit—the world's tiniest woman. Sharky and Gnome had drained my wallet of ones, so I stood by as Little Linda disappeared behind a canvas door. She was gone for two minutes, tops. When she exited, she said, "I really wish I hadn't seen that. I feel rude."

I said, "Was she real?"

"Yes. She's 29 inches tall. She was sitting in a chair on top of a table."

I asked, "Did you talk to her?"

"No. She was on her cell phone, so I said, 'It's nice to meet you' and got the heck out of there."

The tiny woman is the real Little Linda, inspiring my friend's nickname. *My* Little Linda also purchased a three-dollar stick of candied bacon. On the scales of justice, shouldn't viewing a human cost more than a piece of brown-sugar-glazed bacon? We thought so.

I recently witnessed a divorce hearing. I came home, called Little Linda, and said, "That judge is horrible!" She asked why I thought so, and I explained, "When child custody is at stake, don't you think the judge ought to sit up straight?" Let's call that judge Comcast, because he sucks.

Speaking of concessions, I call Little Linda's daughter Pit Boss because she manhandles the workers and contents of the school concession stand like a Smoky Mountain woodcarver chainsaws a black bear out of basswood. I do wish she'd choose between food and money; I watched her shove her little hands into the mandatory polyethylene disposable gloves, then buzz around the concession stand, dip popcorn, handle money, eat popcorn, grab Gatorades from the cooler, and again handle money. As a former waitress, I shuddered and shared my wisdom, "Pit Boss, you can't handle food AND filthy money."

She said, "Sure I can. I'm wearing gloves."

Little Linda's husband, Super Tuesday, runs elections in our community. He catches lots of speculation and grief when the droves drive out to vote. God forbid anyone has to wait in line to select the leader of the free world, right? He does a bang-up job but enjoys few compliments. Maybe he should hire the real Little Linda to distract folks from their long waits. Picture it. Heck, advertise it!

Come one, come all adults to vote!

Show starts this Tuesday at the School Gym
8 a.m. to 8 p.m.

Fake your loyalty to a variety of politicians as you step through a spirit tunnel of poster-yielding hecklers.
View amazing graphic designs using only
3 colors: red, white, and blue!

See Tennessee's oldest volunteers!

Watch in amazement as they read size 8 font and work dials with numbers.
Smell the Domino's pizza!
Meet real election commission officials!
Sign your name upside down!
Spend an hour in line as you guess party affiliations of other voters and try to psyche out your opposition.

And, before you slip behind a curtain to cast your ballot, slip behind our curtain to cast your eyes on the world's tiniest woman.

TEACHERS

Many folks, all having *been* students, think they can *manage* students and teach. Doing math and explaining math are very different things. Teachers commit to hundreds of hours of college, graduate school, professional development, and in-service coursework. They spend anywhere between one semester and one year as unpaid apprentices before they can secure jobs.

Tall Child was annoyed at my extensive time on our computer one day. He desperately needed to turn in his fantasy football draft. I desperately needed to plan a real world, Quadrant D, Common Core, computer applications lesson using core content from English I's *Romeo and Juliet*. I needed time; he needed a new running back.

He asked, "Why do you spend so much time on lesson plans? You just do the chapter, do the questions at the end, and get on with it." Not so, my dear.

Don't you think that government officials overuse the education system as a platform to push their ideas and bills? With every governor comes a new standardized testing process. As a student I probably took dozens of different tests under a variety of presidents, education commissioners, governors, superintendents, principals, and teachers. Every test had me read a passage and respond. Every test had me put some kinds of something in sequence. Every test had the same questions. You remember.

1. A man is six feet tall. He casts a shadow that is eight feet long. The tree beside him is twenty feet high. How long is the tree's shadow?

2. Trains A and B leave the station at the same time, going in opposite directions. Train A travels 60 mph while Train B travels 40 mph. In exactly 2.5 hours, what is distance between the two trains?

My sweet friend Agape Agave was almost late to a work appointment on the other side of the county. She joked, "I took Western Avenue to get to Karns. Oh, my, gosh. Don't ever go that way! Two trains slowed me down. Can you believe that? I thought trains were over." Agape, as long as there are standardized tests, there will be trains.

There is great irony in our mutual criticism. My dear old Gatlinburg-Pittman High School band director, Music Man, told me a conversation he overheard while eating lunch at McDonald's. Construction workers sat nearby. One of them said, "I'm doing work for one of them high-falootin' teachers." I think that construction worker needs to cruise through a faculty parking lot. Educated? Yes. Hi-falootin? No.

REALTORS

When Tall Child was a pre-recession realtor, I drove him nuts with my expert advice. I felt my experience in the field equaled his licensure. Before we married, I was 25 and determined to be a homeowner. I bought a house for $74,500 from a calm elderly couple. We negotiated the FHA, THDA, three-percent-down deal with grace. A year later, I easily sold that house to my cousins and used the $1,200 capital gain to fund my wedding. I then sold Tall Child's home to a co-worker. "For Sale by Owner" can be translated, "Stress yourself out as you moonlight a side career and, in the end, make less money."

As I watched Tall Child weave real estate string art between over-emotional buyers, unrealistic sellers, uptight mortgage underwriters, tardy subcontractors, last minute title attorneys, and slow appraisers, I recognized his talent and my deficiencies. I stopped giving him advice, but I did help him. I drove around Knox County and hammered his "For Sale" signs into the ground.

Losing money and wasting time weren't my only mistakes. The lady who bought Tall Child's house called me and said, "Bug, you left a big piece of wedding cake in the freezer. What should I do with it?"

I said, "Eat it on our anniversary, I guess."

Uncle Trout sneaks a sliver
from my groom's cake.

Theory 17: Funerals beat weddings, for guests anyway.

Disclaimer: Like anyone, I hate to say goodbye to people I love. Death may be natural but it is also tragic, unsettling, and sometimes so awful that the painful loss we feel is otherworldly in its scope. I know grief. Delicious and I lost Pooh to a massive heart attack. We miss him every day of our lives. We all know grief. I didn't write this Theory to poke fun at death or grief. In my weird way, I wrote this Theory to encourage readers to be less concerned with the trappings of life, and more concerned with the fleeting moments and loved ones in life.

I hate weddings. Weddings are fairytale endings. Exactly. Endings. Endings to the fairytale and entry into a daily reality of negotiation, submission, patience, forgiveness, tolerance, vulnerability, and commitment. Congratulations! You now have a roommate. For life. So, if you are a gentle *literal* reader, please refrain from our culture's latest hobby—seeking to be offended—until you read this entire Theory. I honor the dead. I hold the covenant of marriage in high esteem. But, there are things to consider. So, read, reflect, and, if nothing else, forgive me as I figuratively walk down the aisle through the valley of the shadow of death.

Woody Allen said, "I'm not afraid to die, I just don't want to be there when it happens." Amen, weird Woody. I wasn't afraid to get married. I just didn't want to be there when it happened. I'm not a delicate flower of the South. I'm feminine and I try to be ladylike, but I'm about as good at table-setting, flower-arranging, dish-shopping, and party-planning as I am at basketball. Tall Child, on the other hand, was raised in church, a country club, and private schools. He is a modern Southern gentleman. He wants to do things "the right way."

I knew we were right for each other, but Tall Child is a procrastinator. I am an activator. I made the same mistake a lot of girls make — I waited for a man's actions to determine mine. After two and a half years of movies and Mexican food, I was weary of waiting for a proposal. Tired of living on the fence and living in a dorm-like domicile (tiny apartment), I decided to buy that $74,500 house. I met with the sellers. We signed a contract. I secured financing.

That evening I went to Bop and Boss Hog's house for dinner with them and Tall Child. I arrived first, and I told his parents my exciting news. Later, when Tall Child walked into the living room, Bop said, "Son, Bug bought a house today!"

Tall Child said, "What!?! How did that happen? You didn't take me with you to see it or even ask me about anything."

I said, "Why would I? You are my 36-year-old *boyfriend*."
Ouch.

Tall Child's hurt reaction gave me hope, but I saw no traction toward marriage. Not long after that, it dawned on me how to close the deal. Again, I went to his parents' house for supper, and got there before he did. Bop asked, "Why did you decide to buy that house single and so young?"

I explained, "I'm a grown-up. It's a good investment. I'm young, I'm sick of living in a Rubik's Cube, and I'm moving forward in case Tall Child never asks me to marry him. I have to take care of myself." *Bait.*

She said, "Well, he was married before you know. He's gun shy."

I said, "Well, if he doesn't realize how exceptional I am, I'll probably lose interest before he becomes un-gun shy." *Open the bail. Cast.*

She said, "Well, he loves you. You need to be patient."

I said, "Bop. Do you want grandchildren? Dogwood Deb doesn't seem to be in a hurry. J-Bird isn't married and lives a fantastic life traveling the world. I, on the other hand, want three children. I plan to try to get pregnant as soon as I'm married." *Close the bail. Set the hook. Reel.*

One month later, Tall Child invited Delicious and me to his parents' home for Christmas Eve dinner with his entire family. We accepted.

Tall Child loves holidays, so it didn't surprise me when he saw me happily decorating my little house and asked to borrow some Christmas baubles for his. He specifically asked for a stocking.

I said, "Who is going to fill it? You live alone."

"Just for looks," he said.

I loaned him a long, skinny, striped knit stocking.

Then, I remembered that Bop and Boss Hog gave their grown children stockings. I figured they needed one more since I'd be there that year.

I don't mean to brag, reader, but this is important: I often solved the crime before Jessica Fletcher did. I daydreamed, *If I were the writer, in the last episode of "Mad Men," Don Draper would create the Coca-Cola ad where the hippies sing "I'd like to teach the world to sing...."* In other words, I'm hard to surprise. And, dang it, I didn't tell Tall Child my Mad Man concept until we saw the final episode, and it HAPPENED exactly that way. He suspects I am fudging. I'll never convince him. I'm no soothsayer, but, the clues added up:

Clue #1 - He borrowed one stocking from me.

Clue #2 - They invited my mother.
Clue #3 - My cousin called me and told me to make sure I looked good for pictures.
Clue #4 - When Delicious and I arrived, I spotted a video camera on the coffee table.

Then, I spotted my stocking. There it hung from Bop's garland-laden mantle. Picture a Grinch-like, undernourished woven sock. With a square toe. No, make that a CUBED toe.

Mama was a "Murder She Wrote" mastermind, too. The moment she spotted that cube-toed sock, she gave me a wide-eyed stage mother glare and whispered, "Put on some lipstick."

She understood that her mad lib daughter was about to have to give a prim and proper performance.

I wasn't nervous. I was amused.

Bop served us cocktails and appetizers. We all chitchatted for a while, and I received a disproportionate amount of attention. Finally, my on-schedule father-in-law brought things to order. "Let's have the children open their stockings," commanded Boss Hog.

I'd already Jessica Fletcher'd the outcome, so I decided to mess with them.

"I'll go first!" I said. A, loud unanimous, "NOOOO!" from Tall Child's clan rattled Bop's Lenox Holiday china.

Dogwood Deb said, "Let's draw numbers."

The clan said, "Good idea."

Dogwood Deb quickly scratched numbers 1, 2, 3, and 4 on individual slips of paper. She then folded each slip and placed it in a coffee cup and walked into the living room. "Okay, let's draw!"

Obviously they wanted me to go last because that would have been the most dramatic situation. Reader, *obviously*, Dogwood Deb should have written "4" on each piece of paper and had everyone else fib in random order. Instead, they all <u>hoped</u> I would draw number 4. They had a 25-percent chance of an ideal outcome. We passed the cup.

Tall Child squeezed his manly hand into the coffee cup. 1.

Dogwood Deb drew. 2.

My then brother-in-law drew. 4.

"Ruh-roh."

I drew the last slip of paper. 3.

This is too funny, I thought.

Immediately, Dogwood Deb interjected, "You know, Bug should go last. This is her first Christmas Eve with us!"

"No, no. Fair is fair. Brother-in-law drew the 4. He gets the grand finale," I said.

Tall Child and Dogwood Deb quickly emptied their stockings of knick-knacks and candy.

Suddenly, attention turned to me. Tall Child brought me the stocking. Dogwood Deb fired up the video camera. Bop and Delicious watched with Proton therapy focus. I expressed thanks as I pulled out candy bars and treats. Everyone laughed when I lifted a roll of stamps and a tiny box of Tampax Pearl tampons from the sock. You see, weeks before, Bop asked me, "What do you want for Christmas?"

I said, "Ugh. I don't know. I'm good." I love Jesus, but I don't love Christmastime.

She asked, "Well, what is something you need, but don't like to buy for yourself?"

I said, "Stamps and tampons."

So, every year, she gets me a roll of stamps and a box of name brand tampons.

Okay, back to the story.

I slowly extracted Doublemint gum, Snickers, Twix and laid them on the sofa cushion beside me; I didn't put things in my lap because I knew I'd soon have to stand. Finally, after three years of ultimatum-avoiding courtship, my fingers touched velvet. I drew my future from the bottom of the stocking.

He looked at me. Everyone looked at me. Dogwood Deb's video camera malfunctioned, so she put it down and looked at me. Bop said, "Well, Tall Child, honey, ask her."

"I love you. Will you marry me?"

"Yes."

Delicious rejoiced, "BUG! HOW DO YOU *FEEL*?"

I said, "Relieved. Tall Child is my hero."

Whaaaaaaaaaat?

It never occurred to me to rehearse my reaction to Tall Child's proposal. It never occurred to me that I would be center stage and give a press conference right after the match. I guess what I *meant* to say or *should* have better articulated was, "I am relieved and thankful to have found someone so patient, masculine, laid back, handsome, and hard-working who understands me, respects me, and loves me as much as Tall Child does. Tall Child is my hero because I battle severe anxiety and he can actually calm me. Plus, he loves Mexican food and The Tams, and he weighs more than I do."

Although that proposal was funkily coordinated, and certainly not private, I wouldn't change a thing. You marry the family, so you might as well let the family propose. They were all so proud and happy. And, I *was* relieved. I was finally liberated from romance limbo.

That was Friday. Saturday, I pleaded, "Tall Child, let's get married at the beach by ourselves on our honeymoon and come back and throw a big backyard barbeque blowout with a band." (I like simplification *and* alliteration.)

Tall Child said, "No way, Bug! This is your *first* wedding."

???

I was madly in love with Tall Child. I was absolutely ready to be a wife, but I had absolutely zero interest in being a bride.

My happy-go-lucky Tall Child didn't understand me at the wife level just yet. How could he? We didn't share bills, own a pet together, touch each other's money, or live together.

You see, I've suffered off and on from depression and anxiety since my father's premature death. He was 44. I was nineteen. I hate to be forced into formal situations. I don't mind being the center of attention, and I enjoy speaking in public, where I can set a casual tone. But weddings put so much pressure on the bride to be mannerly and formal and skinny and perfect. I was, and am, none of those.

Actually, my three best friends in high school and college (Mare, TRO, GT) and I made a pact to never require each other to be bridesmaids — mountain girls don't care for pomp and circumstance. Mare married in Vegas. TRO jetted off to Houston, Texas, to be a chemical engineer and got married there. GT snuck into a church on a Thursday and wrapped up her nuptials. I was the only one to break the pact. GT stood by me. She was beautiful.

I've had to participate in only one wedding. I was old, married, and a mother, so I told the bride, "I *will* wear a bra, no matter what kind of dress you put me in." She backed off the bridesmaid campaign and assigned me to read from the Bible. I was relieved, until I read the passage, where one portion really, ahem, *stood out*:

"My beloved is like a roe or a young hart: behold, he standeth behind our wall, he looketh forth at the windows, shewing himself through the lattice." (Song of Solomon 2:9)

Song of Solomon is beautiful, romantic, and passionate. I freaked out. I worried I'd trip up on some words. I lamented my concerns to my buddy RokNVol, who would be at the wedding. I read her the passage. She cracked up at my dilemma. Then she said, "The *moment* you say, 'shewing himself through the lattice' I'm going to snort from my pew!"

I rehearsed. And rehearsed. At the actual rehearsal, the priest pulled me aside and handed me an abridged reading. No "shewing" on his sheet — yay! I guess that sexy sentence was too clinical for the cleric.

I made it through with no glitches or snorts. Whew. I have to say, as pretty as that wedding was, the highlight of the weekend occurred after the rehearsal dinner. We all went to a karaoke bar in the lobby of a Gatlinburg hotel. My tall, boisterous family took over the joint. Late night, Tall Child whispered to me, "Let's sing a duet." I was shocked. Then I decided to shock the crowd. I stealthily selected a song and asked the DJ to announce us as "The Dyers." A few songs later, the DJ called into the microphone, "Let's have The Dyers come on up."

Family and friends freaked when they saw Tall Child take center stage. Then, we brought the house down with Tim McGraw and Faith Hill's "Let's Make Love." We didn't do the lift, but we got a standing ovation.

Back to my story now. Tall Child proposed on a Friday. I made a list on Saturday:

- *Call the church* on Monday and ask the pastor for his first open Saturday morning wedding slot — cheaper, simpler, quicker. He told me April 15 was open. I said, "Book it for 11:00 a.m." Check!
- *Call the bank's caterer* and asked him to fax me his wedding menu. I circled what I wanted and faxed it back. Check!

- *Register for china.* Delicious and I went to Dillard's home department. I chose inexpensive dishes from the floor-to-ceiling shelves, walked up to the registry clerk, and said, "I need to complete a bridal registry."

She asked, "Do you have an appointment?"

I said, "No ma'am. I don't need one." I gave her the names of the everyday and formal patterns and asked her to "put me down" for twelve place settings of each. Oh, and some white towels.

Days later, my mother-in-law, the ultimate Southern hostess, said to me "Bug, I looked at your registry. Why didn't you select a coffee maker?"

I said, "I don't drink coffee."

Clueless bride? Check!

The night before our wedding, I did not sleep. After a long evening of nervous twitching, I took a shower, slapped on my grocery store make-up, and headed to the big city of Knoxville to get married. I made Delicious whip me through Burger King for some Cini Mini's.

In the church's bridal suite, which doubles as the vacation Bible school hospitality room, I put on my lovely and wonderfully borrowed wedding dress, popped half a Klonopin from Delicious's jeweled handbag, and got myself hitched. The entire ceremony took 10 minutes. Delicious timed it for me. Check!

Better yet: Check! *Mate!*

Here's my take on how funerals are better than weddings, for the guests, particularly in the South, by category, for my particular and perhaps peculiar self. Note the parallelism as you read.

Planning

Weddings

Wedding planning can take a long time, depending on the wedding couple's families, social status, connections, and wealth. And all that time is a petri dish for rapid growth of stress cooties, cash cooties, and gossip cooties, all of which multiply exponentially. No, wait, cells divide to increase, right? Either way, the longer the engagement, the larger the emotional and financial price tags. My cousin A-Boo is in her mid-30's. Her international business career requires her to live in different parts of Europe and Canada. A few months into her engagement to handsome Scotland native, Jipper, I asked my smart, busy, globe-trotting cousin, "How are the wedding plans going?"

She said, "Much better now that I cut out the middleman."

I asked, "Who's the middleman?"

"Me," she said.

It was too much of a hassle to plan a Seale, Alabama, wedding for an American and a Scot who were living in London. In January 2016, A-Boo and Jipper tied the knot on a ski trip to Steamboat Springs, Colorado. Apparently, Colorado is the perfect locale for a destination wedding. I knew I should have learned to ski when I lived in Gatlinburg!

A quick engagement is ideal, because all that time between the engagement and the wedding allows too much time for thinking. There's always the risk of a reconsideration and a breakup. Consider movies like *The Notebook, Sweet Home Alabama,* and *Runaway Bride*. Married ladies, don't tell me it didn't cross your mind! Don't tell me you *never* dream about your college boyfriend. Of course, pre-wedding dreams are innocent compared to pregnancy dreams. Top secret stuff, right mamas?

Funerals

Unless your family has one of those open or closed casket battles, funeral planning often goes quickly. Either the deceased has total control via written instructions, an assertive relative takes the lead, or the left-behind family collaborates. The funeral directors that I know pray with families. Wedding planners probably should do the same.

Some folks plan and pay for their own funerals. I'd like to study that concept further, as I've been formulating my own funeral plan for some time.

Tall Child can't handle such depressing talk and usually begs, "I'm having a *good* day, so if you want to talk about stuff like [death, illness, gutters, plumbing, insurance, car payments, resumes, tuition, yellow jacket nests, tax returns, colonoscopies, etc.,] please call your mother." So, how about I document my preferences here? That way, it's public and published, and thousands of people can make Tall Child mind me beyond my grave.

My funeral should be held at Sequoyah Hills Presbyterian Church. If, by the time I die, I've been kicked out, have it at First Baptist Church in Sevierville. Don't ask anyone to write any essays or eulogies. My friend and pastor, Bolt, should apply his eloquent literary skill and Sullivan's Island drawl to comfort the mourners and reassure them of eternal life. Bolt, see if you can beat my wedding record, and do the whole service in under ten minutes.

No casket at the funeral. If I'm in heaven, there's no need to see my body in a box. This is both spiritual and economical. Since no one will see it, buy a cheap box; cardboard is fine. It will help nature along. Ooh, if I *ever* get a new refrigerator, I'll save that box. Take it to the department store and make those customer service grouches wrap it in polka-dotted paper. Green is my favorite color.

Hmmm. What to wear...?

My Owl Squad girls had a lengthy conversation and made inebriated vows to bury each other in bikinis because none of us will wear them now, except for Elaine. *Actually*, because it's such an anomaly to don a string bikini at her age, she wears the most obnoxious ones she can find. Last year, at Edisto Beach, she performed what I can only call her "spider dance" atop a picnic table in the strangest swimsuit I've ever seen. It was some blend of plastic and nylon, screen-printed with an Asian lady's face. Hey, as Buddy always said, "If ya got it, flaunt it!"

So, put me in a bikini, in a sealed box, wrapped in pretty paper. I'd also like some creature comforts: a pillow, a quilt, a bottle of Pinot Grigio, a box of Little Debbie Swiss Cake Rolls, red lipstick, my bear whistle (thanks Downton Gams) and pictures of all my friends and family. Is it strange that I fear being buried alive? I said to Delicious one day, "Mama, I am terrified that I won't be all the way dead when I'm buried."

She said, "I doubt you'll survive the embalming process."

Maybe I don't need that bear whistle.

Don't feel pressured to visit the six-foot rectangular hole again. I won't be there.

If that's too much money and effort, cremate me. There's a place in Blount County that does cremation. I know the director and one of the actual *technicians*. She is sweet. I trust her. I don't want to use the other guy who does the burning. He is six feet eight inches tall and has a temper. Let's call him Lurch. Lurch also cremates pets as a side business. Well, a client brought her precious parakeet in for cremation and handed Lurch a tall, beautifully crafted ceramic urn. Lurch did his job. He placed the four-ounce bird in the 23,000-pound machine, called a *retort*. Moments later, he stomped into the crematory director's office, thrust a teaspoon of ashes toward his boss, and yelled, "Look at this tiny pile of sh*t! What in the f*ck am I going to tell this lady?"

Put *my* ashes in Smoky Mountain pottery, hand signed by the artist. Please, no mass reproduction. Buie, Alewine, or Pigeon River will do just fine. Then, take that pottery to the one-lane bridge at Metcalf Bottoms in Gatlinburg, Tennessee. Sing "Victory in Jesus" and sling me over the rail. Sharky has a great arm. He should be the one. Do it when the river is high, after a rain. I hate the idea of some awkward touron on a tube getting wedged between a rock and me.

Speaking of rain, at my funeral, the feature track should be "Smoky Mountain Rain" by Ronnie Milsap. I want Tall Child to reflect on how awesome I was and how fortunate he was to snag a girl from Sevier County. Here are the other songs I want played:

"When I Get Where I'm Going" – Brad Paisley and Dolly Parton

"I Can Only Imagine" – Mercy Me

"I Saw the Light" – Hank Williams

For those songs, please play the original recordings. Again, no mass reproductions, and please, no amateurs. Somebody find the ghetto blaster on my back porch and bring it. You will definitely need to stop at Walgreens for batteries. Or bring an extension cord.

Hire a blue grass band from East Tennessee led by my gifted mandolin-playing friend Curtis Loew. Organs and pianos depress me. Yes, I know I'll be "gone," but the Baptists say there's no loss of consciousness, so I'd like to think I'll hear the music, too. To Curtis Loew's mandolin, add guitar, dulcimer, fiddle, dobro, and banjo to play me out. Their list:

"Come thy Fount of Every Blessing"

"Let Us Break Bread Together"—This one is my favorite hymns. It was our UT marching band warm-up song. I remember playing it at sunrise, listening for sharps and flats, and thinking how perfect its sweet, humble, communal lyrics and melody are.

"When the Roll Is Called Up Yonder"

"When We All Get to Heaven"

Finally, I want the whole crowd to sing "Meet Me There."

After that, meet each other at El Charro. Be sweet to each other, drink up, and celebrate the fact that our separation at death is temporary.

If El Charro has moved, party at my house and have Jose and the guys cater it. Full bar.

I like when the deceased's photos are displayed, so I want *lots* of pictures. Except, I don't want pictures of me. Instead, I want pictures of the people I love. You are my family, my friends, my life, so you should be honored for tolerating me. You'll find plenty of pictures on my den bookshelves, in the guest room hope chest, and in my nightstand.

Mini-Theory: The photographs in a person's home reveal her ego. Twelve bridal portraits and no framed mother-in-law in sight? Uh-huh. When you next Windex your 12x14 self-portrait, you should wipe down your Big Green Egg and Yeti cooler, too.

Okay…enough about me; I sound like a corpse-zilla!

Dress Code

Weddings

Etiquette dictates that we follow a dress code. Wedding guest dress codes vary. As a Faded Glory label enthusiast, I struggle.

Casual: *How* casual? Should I congratulate you then go mow my yard?
Dressy casual: *How* dressy? Capris with chandelier earrings? If so, Delicious has fifty combos.
Business casual: If I'm careful at lunch on Friday, I can wear my work outfit again at the Saturday nuptials.
Semi-formal: Put on a bunch of fancy stuff, then take half of it off?

I won't bore you with the trite woes of bridesmaids' dresses. The fact that bridesmaid frustration is cliché says enough. Thankfully, some brides are wising up. Instead of forcing their sisters, cousins, and best friends to dye square toed, chunky heeled, one-inch spinster satin slippers, brides allow individual shoe choice.

I've also seen mixed dresses. For those of us who have *no* choice where bras are concerned, dress choice a godsend.

Brides historically fret, fantasize, and celebrate wedding dresses. So much so that a hit TV show was born – "Say 'Yes' to the Dress." Brides don't say "buy." They say "find." It elevates the situation, as in "find a husband," "find a job," or "find a liquor store open on Sundays." I didn't have that problem. I borrowed a dress. I guess I'm not TV material.

Funerals

While wedding "Save the Date" cards keep Weight Watchers in business, at funerals, no one cares. No one criticizes the deceased's outfit. We hope. No one feels pressured to fit into a coffin. We hope.

I've attended fancy memorial services and country graveside funerals. I've seen business suits and overalls. More importantly, I've seen a physical demonstration of respect. I think the "all black" with sunglasses look is strictly Hollywood. And I'll never own a black umbrella. Actually, I gave up on umbrellas. Such bondage and responsibility. I get wet. Then I dry out.

The only thing worse than keeping up with an umbrella is wearing a raincoat, or, geez, a poncho. Tennessee fans have the most obnoxious orange ponchos. We look like a stadium of interstate cones. Most of us have that shape anyway; the poncho accentuates it. Ooh, if it rains at my funeral or when you scatter my ashes, someone should pass out UT ponchos!

Go Big Orange!

Vol for Afterlife!

Food

Weddings

God forbid the chicken tenders with honey mustard get cold. Also, there's nothing worse than a dry cake. Brides and their mothers strategize over menu items, placement, display, temperature, cost, quantity, presentation, etc. And, there's the whole "Don't eat until the bride and groom eat" conundrum. I am always amazed at how humans line up for food no matter what time of day it is. I don't normally eat at 3:00 p.m., but if I'm at a wedding, I starve. Maybe I empathize with the skinny bride.

Though I'd already faxed the bank's caterer my wedding food choices—boiled chilled shrimp, pimento cheese sandwiches, chicken salad sandwiches, fruit, cheese, and stuffed mushrooms—Bop insisted we meet with him to discuss the details. I wasn't sure what these "details" would be. I'd already told the caterer cheddar and pepper jack. Bop is an expert party planner and Southern hostess, so I let her teach me. I forced Delicious to go with me because she doesn't hesitate to say "I'm broke as a haint" on cue.

Bop and Delicious were the perfect purchasing balance. We met the caterer in his pretty Victorian home in North Knoxville. He reviewed my choices. All the above, a simple white wedding cake and a small chocolate groom's cake would be total around $700 to feed 100 starving guests. That was my big-ticket item: food.

He asked if we wanted him to bring silverware and china. I said, "Yes." He asked if we wanted napkins with my and Tall Child's names printed on them. I said, "No. Plain white paper napkins are fine."

Bop asked, "Bug, monograms would be cute. Are you sure?"

I said, "I don't want anyone blowing his nose on my new name."

Funerals

No offense to my catering friends, but the best buffet in the world can be found at a rural church. When my precious great aunt, Big Chick, passed away, we loaded up and headed to a tiny Baptist church in rural Georgia. It's so old, there are Confederate soldiers' graves in the cemetery. Those church ladies put on a feast that I can still taste. Chicken and dumplings, cornbread, fried corn, tomato salad, green beans soaked and simmered for hours in salt, butter, and bacon grease, strawberry cake and banana pudding, and on and on and on. What a comfort they and their food were to all of us. A groom's cake at the bottom of a chocolate fondue fountain couldn't even compare to that spread.

Gifts

Weddings

Registries. Gag. If I could go back in time, I would have registered for all kinds of things I now know are crucial for a happy marriage; but how would I know, since those items aren't offered at department stores? Delicious says that you really don't know someone until you are married to him. True. I will add that you really don't know what household items are important until your marriage depends on them. Who cares about plates and forks? Looking back over sixteen years, I would register for one pair of scissors for each room in the house, jumbo packs of ovulation kits, flashlights, tri-fold poster boards for eventual children and their school projects, twenty sessions with a clinical psychologist, a color printer, a 50-year home warranty, a housekeeper, a weed eater, an indestructible beer cooler, a wine-of-the-week membership, and a lifelong supply of Nair, for two.

With all the shacking up, and people getting married in their thirties and forties, shouldn't couples already have dishes by the big day? Delicious and I find all kinds of cute stuff from Goodwill and Habitat for Humanity thrift stores. Bride, you could throw a whole place setting at your groom and replace it the next day at Dollar Tree. Plan ahead.

When I see young engaged girls with those department store radar guns, shooting away at UPC codes of essential household junk, "Beep, beep, beep," I hear, "Me, me, me." When I see young engaged *boys* with the radar guns, I think one of two things: A) In exactly 40 years, you'll be in this same mall, but in a massage chair waiting for her to pick out orthopedic shoes, or B) As Adele says, you "missed your calling" and she's got a hard row to hoe ahead of her.

Funerals

Deceased people are much less selfish. How often do we read "in lieu of flowers" in obituaries? A donation to Bethany Christian Services or Juvenile Diabetes Research Foundation is a much more meaningful legacy of love than a giant wreath on a tripod.

When Pooh passed away, our small farmhouse morphed into a florist shop. We appreciated the outpouring of love and color. My

UT band director sent a huge basket of orange and white carnations. We were overwhelmed with sympathy and fragrance. After a few days, Delicious couldn't take the shop-smell anymore. Plus, the plants were fading, so we tossed them over the barbed wire fence and watched cows selectively chomp away.

At my death, buy perennials that *you* like. Decorate the church and El Charro; then plant the flowers in *your* yards to remember how much I loved *you*. In lieu of flowers, do whatever you want to do. Delicious says you can't rule from the grave, so I guess I won't.

Photos

Weddings

Even if the pastor says, "Go ahead and eat" in the South (remember, everyone is always starving to death after that twenty-minute ceremony), 500 folks won't touch tongs until the bride enters the reception hall. By the time all those flower girls and ring boys are corralled into decent shots, half the guests have done a few shots of their own, the chicken tenders are cold, and the old people are headed to the door. My favorite wedding picture is of me eating shrimp. What does it say about my wedding that all our photos are candids?

After Dogwood Deb's sweet chapel wedding to my new brother-in-law Randall, Tall Child almost forgot to join the picture-taking. Deb was a good sport. She was an even better sport when the pictures came back. A hole in Tall Child's slacks probably looked like a white dot to everyone else. But, to Tall Child, it was a window into his pelvic region, protected only by his carefully tucked and monitored dress shirt hem. In every photo, his hand covered that tiny hole. It was like a frozen jazz hand. Dogwood Deb cried laughing. I scolded him, "I could have stitched that up. Gnome could have Sharpie'd your shirt tail for you. You *could* have worn underwear."

Funerals

Typically, there are no photo sessions. Yet another reason to sing "Amazing Grace."

Party Atmosphere

Weddings

I've enjoyed some hysterical late-night shuttles back to hotels. Thanks Dot and Boone and friends! But, boy, did I wake up with a headache from all that, um, cake! I've also seen bloody jaws, flying furniture, teetering groomsmen and some moving musical tributes. I'm not a good dancer, but I am a willing dancer. Delicious once said, "Our family is a bunch of loud, outgoing teachers, so everyone expects us to be first on the dance floor. We are expected to be the life of the party." That gets old. Personally, I need alcohol to dance. Do you know what's really sad and awkward? A dry wedding with a live band.

Funerals

There is no pressure to dance at funerals. Honor takes the place of debauchery. In the South, when the grieving family and friends follow the hearse to the graveyard in a long, slow caravan of caution lights and little white flags, other vehicles pull over and stop. Completely. When veterans pass away, a well-earned military salute will do, and folded American flags always put faith, family, and sacrifice in perspective. No one has to do the funky chicken, motion the letters of "YMCA," or, heaven forbid, line dance.

Post-Nuptial/Postmortem Reflection

To illustrate this comparison, I'll simply list sound bites. In other words, these are comments you might hear in car rides home from a Tennessee wedding or funeral.

Weddings

"I thought that one groomsman was gonna pass flat out. He was pasty white up there."

"Who brought that screamin' baby? How rude. My next wedding I'm havin' a nursery in the church basement."

"She'll never be that skinny again. Better enjoy it now."

"What did you call that icing? Fondant? How the hell do you pronounce it? Fond Aunt or Fon don't? It was awful. It looked like pink leather. I know damn well they have cream cheese in Valdosta, Georgia."

"Do you think that band leader was high? He acted high."

"What'd y'all think about the food? They way overpaid somebody."

"Hey, drive through the Krystal. There's nothing worse than being hung over in the morning with a baby to take care of."

"We left early, but who cares? They should have more sense. What kind of nuts get married the same day as the Tennessee-Alabama football game?"

Funerals

"Beautiful service. I loved the music."

"I want [fill in the blank] at my funeral."

"He was such a good person."

"Do you want to go in with me and take them a meal this week?"

"I'm gonna write her a note as soon as we get home."

Reader, I'm sorry if I've perturbed you with this Theory. Perhaps you got married on an SEC Saturday, or your photo session delayed the wedding reception for two hours. It's okay. We all make mistakes, especially in romance. You'll make better decisions next time.

So, when can I pick you up?

Theory 18: Blind dates are the best dates ever!

Let's flash back to a beautiful spring day in 1997. I was performing off Broadway—off Broadway Avenue in Knoxville, Tennessee, that is— as a substitute teller at a bank branch in Halls, Tennessee. I stood in a dusty, paper-littered stable of young women. I counted, keyed, and stamped my way through an ordinary day until the stars aligned, and one casual conversation with a co-worker changed the course of humanity forever.

Luisa Banera Caliente looked over her teller stall wall and said, "I know the perfect guy for you. Want me to fix you up?"

I said, "Sure. Why not?"

Luisa Banera Caliente explained that her husband, The Thoroughbred, had a softball teammate who would like me. She proposed a double-date; I accepted her proposal. Between customer interactions she wooed me for the rest of the day with Tall Child trivia:

"He's tall."

"He has sandy blonde hair."

"Not sure how old he is."

"He's an athlete."

"I think he went to UT."

And so on....

The next week I returned to my normal branch. Luisa sent me a softball team picture through inter-office mail. I'd never dated an athlete, so when I saw his lean form outfitted in red and gray stripes, I was intrigued. Tall Child called me and we talked. I don't recall anything memorable about the conversation, other than he seemed quiet and calm. We planned our double date, but I got sick and had to cancel. Twice. Then I kind of lost interest. Delicious asked me if I was dating anyone. I told her about the fix-up, and that I probably wouldn't go. She said, "Bug, you promised that boy you would go on a date. You are going. Call him back."

I called him and left a half-hearted voice mail, "This is Bug. I feel better now. You seem really nice, so if you still want to meet, call me back." I hope Sharky and Gnome have better game.

Tall Child and I met for dinner at La Paz. He brought married friends Daisy and Bad Bill for backup, in case I was a "dud." Since they were married, and I was twenty-two, I figured they were quite mature and much older. Mature, yes, older, no. I said, "Yes, ma'am" and "Yes, sir" to them all night. With my Appalachian accent and humble speech, I "reckon" they thought I was a hillbilly idiot.

I became intoxicated by Tall Child, then tequila, and the rest is history. Or, was it tequila then Tall Child? Every year on our anniversary I think about that chance assignment with Luisa. She's still Caliente and my friend, as are Daisy and Bad Bill.

I'm a risk-taker, so I never shied away from a blind date. I figured, if the guy didn't call me for a second date, I shouldn't take it personally because he didn't really *know* me; however, my social research confirms that most people hesitate to date strangers. Maybe that's because the whole "Don't talk to strangers" maxim is beaten into our brains. I suppose it should be edited to "Don't talk to strangers…until you are ready to get married and start a family. Then it's okay to talk to strangers."

I loved blind dates because, thanks to my friends and relatives, the boys were pre-screened and pre-qualified. Also, I could be completely myself and have nothing to lose. There was no year-long crush to build up my nerves. There was no miserable love-sick stomachache to battle. There was nothing at stake. If he didn't like me, I could say, "What an idiot" or "I didn't like him" or "He doesn't even *know* me" or "He probably didn't call me again because he probably fell into a sinkhole." There are lots of limestone sinkholes in Tennessee.

Those of us who do meet on blind dates, fall madly in love, and live happily ever after-ish become champions of matchmaking. After Tall Child's and my love match, I felt compelled to pay it forward. After a handful of awkward failed attempts, I struck gold with a match between my dear friend Mint Julep and The Landlord. A whirlwind courtship ensued and now they live fairytale style with two beautiful daughters in a stately home atop a beautiful lawn overlooking the Tennessee River. What if one of their daughters grows up to be the scientist who discovers the cure to something impossible to cure all thanks to my romantic engineering?

My cousin Roscoe was on the MTV show "Blind Date." He's a natural entertainer (should be a game show host) and his very presence soaks up a room. So, he played up his role on MTV with comic passion and flair. Roscoe from Tennessee and the strange girl from California enjoyed massages, wine tasting, and limo rides in Los Angeles. He admitted to me that he kind of liked the girl, but sensed the feeling wasn't mutual. So, when the show's host asked Roscoe, "Now that your blind date with California Girl is over, what do you have to say?"

Most young men are in constant fear of rejection in private. Roscoe was on national cable television. Even though he kind of liked the girl, Roscoe answered to the ego-defending negative. Ever the showman, he wanted to produce good TV so he replied, "I think she should make like Michael Jackson and *beat it*."

I loved to poll my freshmen students. When rough-drafting this Theory, I instructed them, "I'm going to say a phrase. I want you to say the first words that come to mind when you hear the phrase. Girls first. Then boys. Ready? <u>Blind date</u>."

Female students' responses:
Creepsters.
Goobers.
Not safe.
Don't find a date on Craig's List.
Hey! That's how my parents met.
Check him out from a distance so you can make a run for it.
Maybe if he went to band camp he'd be safe.

Male students' responses:
Mysterious lover.
Only if I hear about her from a friend I trust.
Bad idea.
What if she is Amish?
I went on a blind *texting* date.
Act like you are not yourself.
Yeah! You can change your accent with every sentence.
Yeah, be all city-folk then all country and say, "Dad gum!"
Be careful. You don't want to get "catfished."

My buddy Sweater Vest Romeo says, "Blind dates are the best because they can't see what you are doing to them."

I asked Tall Child, "What do think about blind dates, in general?"

My eloquent husband said, "They're good, as long as you get to ...." And now we know why *I* gave The Talk to Sharky and made Tall Child sit and listen.

I understand the hesitation. On the bright side, blind dates can be like toy store grab bags. The enticing toy sacks-slash-humans promise surprises, happiness, and fun. Unfortunately, those bags often bring the proverbial baggage—addictions, hang-ups, annoying ex-spouses, debt, and bad credit. Blind dates are typically associated with negative experiences, but they can work out to wedded bliss.

For this topic, I completed lots of field-playing research before the ultimate blind date experience led me to Tall Child. As I mentioned, I embraced the adventure. That was 20+ years ago, long before online dating was commonplace and social media opened the voyeurism doors for all of cable-connected humanity. Also, thanks to the internet, I was able to find and define different blind date scenarios. Friends mentioned hereafter, *thank you* for letting down your guards so others could see behind the blind date curtain.

THE ACCIDENTAL PERVERT

The one solid college friend I gleaned from four years of higher education is quite possibly the most laid-back human on planet Earth. She suffered a traumatic neck injury in high school and spent months in the hospital. She told me once, "I pretty much died and came back to life, so not much bothers me." I agree. She is and was cool, except that it took her two hours to get ready to "go out" on UT's Cumberland Avenue Strip. Most of that time was dedicated to outfit choice and bangs placement. She was worth the wait, because of her party skills and her handicap tag. That handicap tag dangled from the rearview mirror of an electric blue Geo Storm until she wrecked it into an antique shop on Middle Creek Road in Pigeon Forge. She upgraded to a bright red Camaro. Not bad.

We stepped out of the tagged sports cars to front row parking at our favorite bars: The Lap, The Library, and The Underground. So, we nicknamed her HH. The second H doesn't really fit her, but it sounded good with the first H. I'll let you figure it out. A friend set HH on a blind date with a boy who was from her hometown but was a little younger than HH. Well, she thought, *No big deal. Could be fun.* Naturally, during the date, they talked about their hometown, people they knew, etc. Then she figured out that she used to baby sit **him**. HH finished her supper and the date, and never went out with him again. She said she couldn't get the thought of him being six-years-old out of her head.

HOSTAGE SITUATION

You are invited as a third wheel to a party so you can meet another third wheel of the opposite sex who is "perfect for you."

Stay off the spinach puffs. Wear flattering vertical neon stripes. You may meet your future husband at your neighbor's child's birthday party at Laser Quest. You could stalk the guy down a dark tunnel, shoot him, lunge onto his body, and give him mouth-to-mouth resuscitation. If he objects, simply say, "Oh! Sorry! I thought this was for real."

PREMATURE, UM, COMMITMENT

Lifestar gave guys two good hours. If she didn't like them, she cut their time. One guy proclaimed love at first sight. He said, "You are The One. I want you to meet my mother." She dumped him 30 minutes into happy hour.

Lifestar shared with me her ten requirements for a blind date to progress to a second date:

1. A solid job
2. Must dress well.
3. Must not be married.
4. Must not live with his mama.
5. A decent car. No rattletraps.
6. Fun personality.
7. Handsome.
8. Secure and confident.
9. NO tennis shoes on a date. Gross. Kick him to the curb.
10. Not clingy. Friday night is girls' night.

GO BIG OR GO HOME

My sweet high school friend Punkin told me that after she divorced, a friend tried to help her "get back out there." Punkin was chubby, but her friend promised this guy was "into bigger girls." Well, she met him at a restaurant, and they had a decent time, until the end of the date. He asked her to come back to his hotel and sit on him. Yep. Squish him. My polite friend declined, saying she wouldn't want to hurt him. He begged and asked if she would at least come sit on some furniture and try to break it.

BACK IN THE DAY

In this digital age, complete surprise is almost impossible. But, back in the '60s at The University of Georgia, dating in the dark was par for the romantic course. Now, Delicious was five feet ten inches tall, so her primary concern with blind dates was their height. Other than that, she had no major requirements. She often reminds me that she was super slim in college by bringing out a small shiny alligator-skin belt. Unless I use it as a tourniquet for a zombie bite it serves no one these days.

Delicious asked to explain a typical blind date at UGA. She didn't trust me to accurately articulate the details, so here's her description:

> *At my beloved University of Georgia (I graduated in 1969), I lived on the coolest floor at Rutherford Hall. The Greek revival boasted antebellum columns, wide impressive steps leading to an expansive porch, not inferior to the porches of* Gone with the Wind's Tara *and* Twelve Oaks, *and huge windows. How exciting it was to watch a weejun-loafered, madras-shirted UGA boy bound up those steps at just the time my blind date was to arrive. Bonnie Reed was always my blind date agent. She was a business major, and knew way more cute boys than I, an education major, knew. She fixed up friends like me with great looking hell raisers who appreciated the value of time. You see, we had to get drunk fast to maximize our fun before strict dorm curfews and housemothers interfered. One such blind date asked me, "Do I have something on the side of my face?" and then turned to pop kiss me on the lips as we descended the steps of Rutherford Hall and headed for the beer store. Many boys lived in off-campus dwellings, which co-eds referred to as "wild places." Wow! What great memories I have of Bulldog Trailer Park and Parson's Circle Apartments. And the music in those days was perfect. Otis Redding, The Drifters, The Tams. Really, is there anything better than being twenty-years-old, looking the best you will ever look, sucking down ice cold beer, and dancing the South Carolina Shag to perfection with a handsome blind date? I doubt it.*

ON-LINE-BLIND

Don't be digitally delusional. Caveat! You *think* you saw a picture and had a "conversation" but that bodybuilding thoracic surgeon with no children, no living parents, and a house in Destin, Florida, might be your dry cleaner's teenage son. Or daughter.

A couple of years ago, newly single Dogwood Deb wanted to find true love, and, like other divorced middle-aged mothers, worried that she'd never find her soul mate. But, one day at Bop's house around Easter time, we took a chance and found a prize egg. After a family supper, Dogwood Deb and I indulged in a little (okay, a lot) of Pinot Grigio. She lamented her romance woes. I asked, "But are you taking *action*?"

She said, "I tell everybody to be looking."

I said, "Not enough."

"Well, my best friend did find her husband on the dating site Plenty of Fish."

"Plenty of Fish? Ha! Let's do it!"

"No way."

More wine.

Way.

Dogwood Deb flipped open Bop's laptop and opened a Microsoft Window to her future. She began, "Okay, I need a username. You don't use your real name on Plenty of Fish. I definitely want something that will get guys' attention. What should I call myself?"

I said, "Oh, that's easy. Night Crawler."

CHANCY, BUT LADYLIKE

Tall Child's aunt Ree didn't like working Saturdays, but one Saturday in 1959 began a lifetime of happiness. She was an accounts payable clerk at a Nashville financial institution with Boss Hog. Think cinched waistlines, classic cars, long cigarettes, and manual typewriters. During their overtime weekend shift, Boss Hog said to her, "My brother just came home from military service. I think you two would really get along." Ree gave him her number.

We'll call him Uncle. Ree shared an apartment with other young secretaries. One evening, the telephone rang. Uncle was on the line. Ree spoke with him a bit and agreed to go on a date. Her overprotective, somewhat nosy roommate, whom they called "Mother" for those traits, quizzed her. Ree gave no details. Her tongue was composed, but her mind was flustered. She liked what she heard from Boss Hog and from Uncle, but she also liked tall men. While Boss Hog had considerable character, he was quite slight in height.

When Uncle came to the door, Ree greeted him in flats. He asked, "Are you ready to go?"

She looked up, up, *up* to his sweet face atop a slender build, and said, "Just a minute." She darted to her bedroom, kicked off her flats, and slid into high heels.

They went to dinner at the first Shoney's built in Nashville. The date was going well, so Uncle suggested they go to a movie. Ree agreed. Then, Uncle asked, "Well, we have two choices. The drive-in or the walk-in."

Ree told him, "Well, since we just met tonight, and I don't know you very well, I think the walk-in would be more appropriate."

They saw *Hercules*. Ree told me, "I don't really remember anything about that movie. It wasn't my sort of thing, but I made the wise decision to go to the walk-in theater instead of the drive-in."

They were married 46 years.

Friends, there's really nothing to lose and everything to gain with a blind date. The course of humanity may be changed in an instant when a friend or coworker casually says, "I know the perfect guy/girl for you." Slap on some lipstick/cologne and dream big, as in *big* romance, as in *big* love. Speaking of big love, that reminds me of a Theory my friend Fancy and I share….

Ready for take-off.

Theory 19: All mothers need sister wives.

Let's take it way on back, folks. Way on back to the early 70's in dusty, hot, cotton-dotted Seale, Alabama, to the home of my uncle Trout, where whispers of big love first surfaced. The female grownups, Delicious, Big Booty J, and my aunt Terrific, sat and talked to the tune of cicadas. They chirped their own woes of work, children, and domestic responsibilities into the Southern breeze for hours. All of a sudden, Terrific, then a mid-level banking executive and mother to three student-athletes, pronounced, "I need a wife." Even though I was elementary-age, my little pink female brain's synapses fired. I asked no questions. Her statement required no clarification. I innately understood.

A couple of years ago, my dear neighbor friend, Fancy, called in a tizzy. She is a true character with somewhat unexplainable talents and unique attributes. She is also an esteemed professor, wife to The Gentleman, and mother of three animated busy boys. The conversation went something like this:

Bug: "Hey Fancy, what's up?"

Fancy: "I hate to even ask you this. You can say no, but I am desperate. Oh, and I'll pay you. I will give you cash! And, I will return the favor. And I won't make you pay me. That's how desperate I am."

Bug: "What do you need?"

Fancy: "[Expletive], I need a sister wife, really. I need another woman to live with me and help me every day, [expletive]."

Bug: "What's your pickle?"

Fancy: "Boy #1 has a soccer tournament in Nashville and I need to take him. Boy #3 is staying with my mother, but Boy #2 can't miss his basketball game and my mother can't handle two wild boys."

Bug: "Where's The Gentleman in all this?"

Fancy: "He's going on a golf trip."

Bug: "I'll keep Boy #2, no problem. You don't have to pay me, because I'll surely need help from you soon."

Fancy: "I really need a sister wife. Thanks for being my sister wife!"

Bug: "Ha! I need one, too! But, that's a little kinky and cult-like."

Fancy: "Think how convenient it would be. I need two sister wives, actually—one wife per child."

Bug: "Man-to-man defense. True. Right now you are running a zone. But really, three sister wives could handle twenty children better than one man can 'babysit' his own two or three."

Fancy: "Yeah! Why do the men say 'babysit'?"

Bug: "They simply don't have our natural ability to anticipate the needs of others. It's the same reason most retail bankers, teachers, nurses, and servers are female."

Fancy: "No kidding. You want to be my sister wife permanently?"

Bug: "I don't want to see your husband naked, but I think we could work something out. You are definitely onto something, but I'm not sure I could live with a bunch of women. I think I'd rather have *brother husbands*. I could assign them zones of responsibility and choose them according to skill."

Fancy: "Wow."

Bug: "Please. *Not* the zones you're thinking. I'd marry one plumber, one electrician, one carpenter, one pediatrician, one academic, one party boy, one financial planner, one landscaper, and so on. All relationships, except the one with Tall Child, would be platonic on *my* compound."

Good news! The Gentleman chose, selflessly, to stay home, even though Fancy applied no pouting or pressure tactics. She had the problem solved via her sister wife. It was a miracle in masculinity! Or, maybe he's prematurely morphing into a woman.

Not long before my sister wife convo with Fancy, I spent one night in Nashville. One night. Tall Child stayed home with Sharky and Gnome. Room and board were free — I stayed with Bop — but it cost me two hundred dollars and two weekends of manual labor. Confused? So was I when I walked into my house after a three-and-a-half-hour drive to find the Gnome's black Sharpie ink-work sketched down the hallway, through the den, across two doors, three windows, and one sofa. He even sketched on molding.

Bush was right. Leave no child behind. With a marker and a man. During SEC football season.

The permanent ink was everywhere. First, I lowered the boom on Tall Child, "What the hell were you doing while Gnome was coloring every room in this house?"

"Huh?" (Tall Child buys time by faking that he's partially deaf in one ear.)

Louder, "What the HELL were *you* doing while Gnome colored every freaking surface of this house with a permanent marker?"

"Oh, I didn't know he had a marker. I was watching ESPN. I think I fell asleep."

Then, I calculated the repair cost. I like to complain with quantitative data, and this snafu involved three paint colors.

"Well, I just measured the hallway. Did you know it takes two gallons of paint to cover 650 square feet of wall space? Plus, I'll probably need two coats, AND he colored on the molding. AND, he colored in three rooms. I'll probably spend half my paycheck on paint. You are helping me, by the way."

"I'll help you, baby," Tall Child said.

I wrapped up my tirade with a long, dramatic group lecture to Tall Child, Gnome, and Sharky. Then, I cried—because I was tired. I was <u>tired</u>. I was worn. Slap. Out.

Except for being too tender-hearted to consistently discipline his boys, Tall Child is a great father. The important thing is that Sharky and Gnome were safe and having fun with their sweet daddy who worships them. He works hard, coaches Sharky and friends, shows affection, and supports his children in every way possible. He is not neglectful. He is busy and, sometimes, after a long workday, he lies on the sofa in the luge position: legs out, head on pillow, body straight, arms crossed over his chest. Every now and then, I poke him as I sweep by, just to make sure he's awake. He says he is, but when he gets in the luge, he struggles to keep up with conversations. If I pepper him with questions, he lifts his left eyelid and mumbles. He wakes up only if I change the channel from SEC Network to Bravo or E!

Look, I make mistakes all the time. But I am 100 percent sure that if the roles were reversed, the Gnome wouldn't have caused so *much* damage. Why? Because, as a female, I know better than to lie down before my boys do. I am woman! Hear me roar, not snore!

Tall Child heard me roar that day.

Here's the conundrum many women face: We need a task to be done, not because we are lazy or incompetent, but because we are busy doing something else. Someone needs to call the insurance company. Someone needs to wait for the plumber. Someone needs to help with homework. Someone must fabricate a science project to look like an actual experiment took place over three weeks' time. Luckily, my housekeeping skills make different stages of mold easy to scrape up.

Women need security. We need action! If we "over ask" our husbands with "honey-do lists" we feel like nags. If we don't "over ask" the task often doesn't get done, or we have to do it, in five-minute increments because we are everyone at once, all of the time.

Tall Child did, indeed, help me clean up the mess Gnome made. Once I identified the paint colors, drove to Lowe's on Saturday morning (children in tow), bought the paint, brushes, and painter's tape, fed everyone lunch, lined up all the supplies, and handed Tall Child a brush and an old plastic coffee can for his paint, he pitched in. One common synonym for "wife" is "helpmate." I helped Tall Child help me paint. Then, one day, he went to his friend Tomcat's house to watch football, and I finished the job, willingly. The boy loves football. And Tomcat made chili; Tall Child loves chili. I was a wife and a helper and happy to spare him the work.

My old friend Lake Girl boycotted her sink and dishwasher for two weeks to see if Lake Boy would notice the growing pile of crusty china. Nope. Fed up, she woke super early one morning, and put every plate, cup, glass, pot, pan, and piece of silverware in the driver's seat floorboard of his truck. He became a visual learner.

One January, I hosted a baby shower for a friend. Bop insisted I have ample seating, so I borrowed 30 folding chairs from a church, on the promise that her darling Tall Child would pick them up and return them after the shower. The following May, I was a about to host a baby shower for a cousin. I hadn't used those chairs for the friend's shower, and I hadn't had the vehicle or the time to return them. (Tall Child faltered on his promise.) The chairs were stacked on our front porch for four months. Inspired by Lake Girl, I moved each and every one into Tall Child's small closet. He, too, became a visual learner.

My precious neighbor Auntie Mame dared me to date items Tall Child left on the porch. I accepted. When I spot a giant gas station Styrofoam cup, a wood sample from his office, the Roundup weed killer, a random storm door leaned against a post, or a half-full, slimy cooler on the porch, I write the date on a piece of paper and tape it to each annoying object. I hope the visual aids will urge Tall Child's left brain to communicate to his right brain and do something. You know—the whole action and consequence concept that men seem to miss. Not long ago, I explained to Little Linda that I was conducted a test. I said, "Tall Child left a Chick-fil-A cup on the top step on our porch. I am leaving it there to see how long he will walk by it. It's a test."

She said, "How long has the cup been there?"

I said, "Two weeks."

She said, "The test is complete. Throw that cup away."

Ladies, can you imagine coming home from work without making a single stop? Can you imagine dropping your car keys on a table and sitting down? Imagine…

No depressing envelopes from the mailbox to open.
No obligatory pull toward the kitchen mess.
No scanning the room for objects to pick up and redistribute.
No whining from the peanut gallery.
No mental math homework or online school stuff to decode.
No onions to chop and make you cry.

I'd *love* to walk into a clean house, see supper cooking on the stove, pour a glass of Pinot Grigio, and relax into the luge position. I just can't figure out a way to beat myself home.

Can I get an "Amen" sister wives?

I warned you that I may vent. But, sister-wives share, so, in that vein, I asked members of my coven, I mean, circle of friends, this question: *Wives and mamas, I want to know what you think. This is your chance to let off some steam, anonymously, of course, so that you can say to your husband, "Hey, look what that crazy Bug and her friends wrote. Can you believe them?" So, if you had a sister-wife, what would you have her do?*

They responded with great passion. Here are all of our answers, with mine mixed in; and I'm not saying which are which from *this* witch:

She would listen to loud, terrible music and talk about American League baseball.

My sister wife would follow [husband and child] around and pick up all the piles of junk they leave in their wakes, make the beds, and remind them of all the stuff they need to do.

Foot rubs, for me.

I'd have her discuss the budget and monthly spending with my husband. Prerequisite: hostage negotiator training.

She would babysit my kids overnight when I travel for work.

Mine would nag the kids to do their stuff, point out to the husband when he's wrong or being a jerk, check the kids' bags before they leave so they have what they need each day, watch football with him, and get up early to wake the kids up. Awesome.

I would send her to the grocery store.

I would gladly forfeit my shotgun seat so she could be the one who jumps in and out of the car to see "how long the wait is" at restaurants, get the mail, stand in line at Bruster's for ice cream, and take the children into gas stations to tee-tee.

My sister wife would change every diaper – from babies to geriatric in-laws.

She'd do the suppositories.

Yeah... I want one to cook, one to decorate, one to clean the house, and one to do my hair and nails. Of course I could use one good gay guy for all of it.

If I had a sister wife, she would get my ignorant ex-husband out of my life, get pregnant, and deal with his crazy first wife forever and ever.

She would clean and do laundry, but I am the ONLY one having a relationship with my man.

Substitute teach for me and be my teacher assistant every day! And fix my hair.

She would do all manscaping to include ear hair, nose hair, and back hair.

If I had a sister wife she would be solely responsible for calling all 1-800 customer service numbers.

Iron.

If my sister wife would run the activity shuttle, unload the dishwasher, and make all appointments, I would be perfectly happy to help with homework, have sex (yes, I said it) at least five times per week, put my babies to bed every night, make dinner, cheer at games, ride in the golf cart, etc. I love the quality time activities but detest the fact that all of the superfluous stuff leaves little time, energy, and patience for it.

She needs to have a job.

If I had a sister wife, I'd probably never come home.

She would have all nighttime responsibilities for all babies.

I'd want the sister wife to be the <u>favorite</u> wife.

One succinct friend said, "The thing with a sister wife is . . . I don't think you would have to *make* her do anything. Women just get things done."

I have to wonder how many households pay for lawn care but don't pay for a housekeeper.

I suspect it's part of the "bro code." Our lawn guy charges $60 a month. A housekeeper would be at least $200. Guess which one we don't have?

Tall Child *does* do the laundry. And, as he does it, he reminds me to thank him. He carries heaping baskets of hot socks and towels down the hall, and says, "Thank you. You're welcome." Once, as cousin A-Boo and I slurped Bloody Mary's on the sofa, Tall Child strutted around with a broom, swept under our feet and bragged, "Look who's doing all the work while you two losers sit there and run your mouths."

A-Boo said, "Yep, You're a real winner. Why don't you run a victory lap around the house? We'll take our drinks outside and watch."

The silverware tray inside the silverware drawer is stupid. I poke my fingers on sharp tines when I unlatch the little silverware stalls. Usually, the gate falls off, and metal pieces crash into the bowels of the dishwasher. Then I have to work a puzzle to get the little plastic boy parts back into the plastic girl parts of the basket. You know the drill. Exhausted, I had an epiphany as I lifted that contraption out of the dishwasher door to go sort silverware: *Why sort at all? How much time am I spending every day sorting cheap metal? I quit.*

I do hide the knives in my spice cabinet. After that, I dump all contents of the silverware basket into the silverware drawer. Tall Child saw my new system and complained, "Why did you do that?"

I said, "Because I am too smart and too busy to waste time separating silverware. It's stupid."

He said, "You are crazy. How will I get what I need?"

I said, "Really? You'll figure it out the first time you eat cereal with a fork."

Another reason I quit sorting is because I want to limit my time with that specific drawer. Two summers ago, I opened it to find a baby copperhead coiled up and ready to kill me dead. Tall Child said it wasn't a copperhead. I said, "Well, it had a copperhead effect on me."

Bop asked, "Why would a snake be in your silverware drawer?"

I said, "It was probably there for the mice."

Male readers, don't dump me. I love you! Your women love you! We want to spend time tied to *you*, not online textbooks and mindless chores. Think *Jerry McGuire*: Help *us* help *you*! Help us help you, so we can show you the money!

Ladies, have you ever felt like you were swept off your feet and then handed the broom? What are you supposed to do? Hand the broom back? No! He's not going to sweep, at least, not when you want him to. I say you dump the silverware and toss the broom. Better yet, get on it and ride. Ride, sister wife, ride! "I believe you can fly. I believe you can touch the sky!" I believe you can ride, or fly, all the way downtown and meet your sister wives around a cauldron of salsa with little mini-cauldrons of tequila for an old-fashioned girls' night out. A night of forgiveness, carbohydrates, cheese, alcohol, understanding, and rest. All of which we desperately need and deserve.

Gnome swings through his baby powder sand trap.

Theory 20: Never call a woman fat, lazy, or selfish. Them's fightin' words.

Why do women scrutinize each other and themselves? Is it cultural? Or is it *natural* to do so? At this point, I want to make something clear; I write from my middle-aged, *married*, working mother perspective. I do not address single parenting for a couple of reasons. First, I cannot comprehend the exhaustion single mothers face on a daily basis. Second, I can't adequately describe the parenting-times-two, physical, mental, and emotional workload you carry. It would be disingenuous for me to even attempt to understand and articulate how much you do for your children. You have my respect.

You calling me FAT?

Sharky's favorite "Yo Mama" joke is *Yo mama so fat, she jumps up in the air and gets stuck.*

I admit. It's funny.

Here's a good middle school retort for that, ladies. Use at will: *I may be fat, but you're ugly, and I can go on a diet.* —W. C. Fields

No, that's mean. Don't say that. Instead, let's be as kind to one another as we hope our waistbands are after a weekend on a houseboat.

There is not an overweight woman on Earth who doesn't know that she is overweight. She never needs nor will she act on cruel admonishment. Delicious once refused to weigh at the gyno's office because she and I were going to Calhoun's Barbecue Restaurant for lunch afterward, and she didn't want to feel badly when she ordered the pork plate.

Delicious told me, "The problem is that I eat like a college athlete, but there was no Title IX back in my day, so I never *was* a college athlete."

Every time Adele eats something she's "not supposed to eat," she humorously growls, "Big girl hungry." Adele is a lovely pale-eyed blonde. She's fit and feminine. She should feel beautiful, but the world convinces her to be self-critical.

Here's my beef. I get hungry. I have a huge appetite for food and life. I associate food with mood. Don't you?

When I feel sad, I crave chocolate. *Warm* chocolate. If I don't have the ingredients for lava cake, I make one of those diet crushing microwave chocolate mug cakes. Some pre-menstrual desperate woman came up with that. I'm sure. That lady did us no favors. I don't know if I should slap her or hug her. Can you imagine the hissy fit that produced such a sweet genius concoction?

When I feel anxious, I crave Barefoot Pinot Grigio paired with chicken and dumplings and fried okra.

When I feel excited, I sear ribeye steaks and whip up Velveeta macaroni and cheese. And fried green tomatoes. And blackberry cobbler.

Children's birthday parties are almost as torturous as outdoor weddings. Is it bad that, after 90 minutes of Jump Jam hysteria, where all I do is eye my child's neck to make sure it's not under another child's foot, I get in line for cake? I earned it, right? Give me the corner piece, please.

Speaking of sweets, my niece Cake must feel the same way I do. She's a middle-schooler who hates to dress up, so weddings and parties are a drag. But, she knows the silver lining of any cloud is laced with sugar. At a cousin's wedding, she asked the family, "Is there going to be dessert?"

I said, "Usually, at weddings, there's some sort of cake." We laughed. She didn't.

When I'm stressed out at work, whatever carbohydrates a vendor or customer brought to our break room will do. Brownies, bagels, candy—anything but fruit.

After almost twenty years of marriage, Tall Child gets it. One morning, we argued. I was hurt. He later called me at my office and said, "I'm bringing you lunch. I love you." He brought me a pint of chocolate ice cream and a plastic spoon.

Adele and I discussed this topic, and she reminded me that women not only associate food with mood, but we also tie certain cuisine to certain events. Do you?

Road Trips

As I type this, Delicious and BBJ are road-tripping to Sikeston, Missouri, to attend the Boot Heel Rodeo with their best friend, First Lady. I sent a text at 8:14 a.m. to wish them a great trip, and Delicious replied, "BBJ and I are eating chocolate chip gooey bars. We have our margarita stuff with us."

Movies

How much *will* you spend for boxed candy and giant Cokes? Adele reported, "No limit. My dates pay for it."

Is junk-food-eating such a movie habit that you resort to smuggling? How far will you go for your routine fix? Grandmama Buddy didn't like junk food and she was an excellent southern cook. She snuck fried pork chops and cornbread into the movies. Before we all had children, my cousins and I and whatever plus ones we'd procured went to the movies every Christmas Day night. Tall Child loves super salty tortilla chips with hot yellow "cheese." One

Christmas night, as we flipped down padded seats and settled in to watch previews, Tall Child dropped his little nacho cheese cup.

"Oh, no! Way to choke," I laughed.

He looked at me with a cocky grin, reached behind him, whipped out a spare cheese cup, and quipped, "Who's your daddy?"

Ballgames

As a daughter, sister, and grandmother to athletes, Delicious has toted her pocketbook to hundreds of concessions stands. Her hoopster-loving habit? Popcorn. Delicious rates popcorn on salt, crunch, butter, and overall value, as in "That bag was *not* worth a dollar." Since she's a retired English teacher, I'll toss out an analogy.

Delicious is to popcorn as a sommelier is to wine.

Whenever Sharky's Knox Sox baseball coach The Best made the post-practice announcement, "We play at Halls this weekend," the parents yelled in unison, "Yes! Fried baloney sandwiches at the concession stand!"

I know it's spelled bologna, but in the South, we say *baloney*.

At the start of every baseball season, my beautiful, fitness-minded friend Friskey on Water proclaimed, "I made myself a rule this year. No concession stand food." She also does tricep dips on bottom bleachers and actually runs during her lunch breaks. Her strong legs give her remarkable balance on boats.

Beach

My staples are Lay's Potato Chips and Mayfield's onion dip, paired with vodka, cranberry, and lime. Tall Child likes Doritos with Mich Ultra.

I am the head cook in my galley, which means I plan, buy, load, unload, cook, and clean up anything to do with food for my family. I'm Southern, which means I like my plate piled up with rich, fried, flavorful food. So, color and taste and texture are important to me. How can I possibly gnaw on rice cakes and tofu? Forget it. In *Eat, Pray, Love*, the main character says to her friend, about enjoying a pizza in Naples, "I'm tired of waking up in the morning and recalling every single thing I ate the day before, counting every calorie I consumed so I know just how much self-loathing to take into the shower. I'm going for it ... and tomorrow we are going to ... buy ourselves some bigger jeans."

Good stuff, but the director missed the mark. He had size 4 actresses wiggle and squeeze into size 6 jeans. *Not* realistic. I was so disappointed. I wanted to see the actual label "Size 12, Average." I wanted to see renowned actresses slide comfortably into some size 14 britches, dang it, and keep on drinking!

Men, it is so cruel to compare women to other women. Can you imagine what that's like? I have certain natural attributes, but, when they are natural, they typically come with extra curves. My bra is so tight to keep Atlantic and Pacific upright that it squeezes little puffs of fat up and out right at my armpits. Hey, sometimes, in a hurricane, the levies break. My friend Cashmere, a beautiful, soft-hearted, high-end seamstress, worked and worked and worked on constructing, I mean, *creating* a dress for me for a fancy party. Those little fat babies kept pooching out from my wire and nylon levies. Frustrated, Cashmere asked, "Girl, what am I going to do about those?"

I said, "Maybe I can duct tape them somehow, or we could embrace them. You could sign them. Write '*Cashmere was here. And over here, too!*'"

I can honestly say that I don't care when Tall Child is in one of his chunky spells. I want him to be healthy, but I certainly don't compare him to a young Robert Redford. That would be ridiculous. Plus, when he's heavier he's slower. I can catch him faster. It's tougher for him to dodge flying Tupperware. And, love handles say he's content, like when skinny people start dating, fall for each other, and chunk up because they are going to restaurants and having fun together.

I usually choke as a dieter. Job stress, writing deadlines, plumbing issues, and Gnome and Sharky's school assignments get the best of me. Maybe I should tell people I take prednisone. Young people, prednisone is a steroid that helps you with all kinds of health problems. It's considered a "miracle drug" but, be careful. A customer warned me, "I used to be purty skinny, but that prednisone blowed me up like a toad."

After a week at the beach, I look like an albino pickle, swollen and softened by seven days in salt water and zinc. Sometimes, I swell right out of my pajamas, which are XL T-shirts and Tall Child's size 42 boxers. Is this why women post only beach pictures of their toes to Facebook and Instagram? I want to see thunder thighs, cankles, and muffin tops. Show me some back fat!

Delicious once said, "I look better 'nekkid' than I do in a bathing suit."

Ditto.

My brilliant beautiful cousin Bags taught me a lesson of self-acceptance when she declared, "I have finally figured out the perfect career for myself. I am going to be a professional 'before' model."

Speaking of naked and modeling, I'm pretty sure I have the perfect body for a toga. I saw a nude of myself. It hangs over the bar at The Bistro at the Bijou on Gay Street in downtown Knoxville. Add a little more up top and the subject could double for me. Instead of nude beaches, there should be toga beaches. You could hog out and take a nap in the same outfit. Bring a cooler and a pillow. I have a new vacation motto: "When in Hilton Head, act like the Romans."

I came up with some good advice a while back, and I encourage you to try it. When you are feeling fat, unsuccessful, or lonely, talk to yourself like you would talk to your son or daughter if he or she were struggling. Tell yourself you are pretty, intelligent, talented, and loved. Even in my tankini at Edisto Beach, surrounded by my gorgeous girlfriends, I tell myself I'm beautiful. Sometimes, I even believe me.

You calling me LAZY?

I don't know a lazy woman. It is impossible to be female and lazy. Delicious claims to be physically lazy, but I think that applies only to housework. She writes letters, as in old-timey correspondence, every day of her life. And she can whip up an original, colorful Christmas wreath in five minutes flat. Delicious and most of her female relatives are teachers. Did you know that teachers, on average, give and receive thousands of verbal and non-verbal responses each day?

Every day I watched Delicious spray up her black curls with lice-fighting Aussie and, in her words, "slap on some Merle

Norman," dress "cheerfully and conservatively with big earrings," and pack a lunch and satchel to teach twelfth grade.

On the way to school, we'd stop for treats and even run errands, but on the way home, she dragged her satchel and never noticed anyone honking at her to budge forward at green lights.

In the halls of Gatlinburg-Pittman, I passed her many times a day. And I watched her eye makeup drain from one class period to the next, so that, by the time we got home, she looked like she had smeared eye-black above her cheeks to block the sun. Your eyeballs can actually sweat. I swear on my teaching certificate.

Toward retirement, Delicious teased her niece, who had also been her student, "You fell asleep every time we watched a Shakespeare movie in class."

The niece said, "So did you."

Delicious said, "That's why I played movies."

She had work napping down to an art. She turned on the VCR, then sat at her desk. She placed the fingers of her left hand across her forehead and held a pen in her right hand, as if she were grading an essay. She leaned over the fake essay and rested her eyes as students "enjoyed" the 1971 production of *Macbeth*. Yes, she took a little break during movies, but before each one, she taught students to really understand Shakespeare and his applications to life. She taught them to respect each other and themselves. She illuminated their worlds with literature and love.

Delicious woke at 5 a.m. every morning for 32 years. She influenced thousands of students. She proofread to the stars and back. She helped Pooh care for a 72-acre farm. She loved my daddy and loves others at a cellular level. She spent time where it mattered: on people, not mindless housework.

When I was a young banker a top female executive told me, "The more successful a man is, the *more* likely he is to have a wife and children. The more successful a woman is, the *less* likely she is to have a husband and children."

Amen. Women carry everything and everyone with them to work. We spend our fleeting lunch breaks on bills, our children, and errands. Tall Child drives through Bojangle's during his lunch break and listens to talk radio.

I recall a particularly stressful morning when Sharky was about eighteen months old and I was a bank branch manager. I woke him up to get him dressed for daycare. His eyes were puffy, and I immediately knew: conjunctivitis. I had a sales meeting at 9:00 a.m. and sales calls scheduled throughout the day. I took Sharky to daycare, drove downtown where my parking spot was two blocks from my office. I parked and pounded pavement to my branch. From my office, I called the pediatrician, who called in a prescription to Walgreens. I waited for Walgreens to notify me that the medicine was ready. Once it was ready, I left my office, hoofed it to the garage, drove to Walgreens, drove to the daycare, put the eye drops in Sharky's pitiful little blue eyes, drove back to the garage, walked back to my office, and plopped, exhausted but on time, into my chair. I led my 9:00 a.m. sales meeting. I couldn't take the day off, and Tall Child was out of town on business. I did it Ginger Rogers style: in taupe heels, pantyhose, and a skirt. Fortunately, our daycare understands the plight of working mothers. They do field trips and breathing treatments and welcome birthday cupcakes. They even host Santa Claus and the Easter Bunny.

I watched an interview with former US Ambassador to the United Nations. Her name is Samantha Power. At the time of the interview she was 43, with two children, ages one and three. She lives in the ambassador's residence at the Waldorf and works fourteen hours a day. When the reporter asked her how she balanced being a working mother, Powers said something like, "Everyone doesn't get 100 percent of me at the same time."

Some of you are thinking, "She is a neglectful mother." Some of you are thinking, "Wow! What a career." I am thinking, "Of course, she had her children later. She had to finish up at Yale and Harvard, build her career, and then start a family."

I like her. She's impressive. But most of my working-mother friends work fourteen-hour days, also. Samantha probably works from 6 a.m. to 8 p.m., but once she's home, she's *available*. Once I'm home, I hesitantly and half-heartedly do the chores her housekeeper does, while my boys play and do homework. No, Samantha probably doesn't pack lunches. My guess is she gets all kinds of perks and time off that her children enjoy. Enough with the working mother guilt. I had the following phone conversation with an elderly, more "traditional" relative:

"Hello?"

"Bug, I was going to leave a message. I figured you would be at work."

"Actually, I took the day off, and I'm picking Sharky up from school right now."

"Oh, look at you, being a real mother today. That's wonderful."

My guess is that anyone as smart as Samantha Power knows precisely how to communicate with her children so that they know she is most definitely their real mother—their real, successful, brilliant mother. My guess is that, if she did pack her children's lunches, those lunches would taste the same as any housewife's children's lunches, depending on the brand of peanut butter.

Let's start a new trend, working and "non-working" ladies. Let's stop being hard on each other. Let's band together and equalize the language. Let's start by calling our husbands "working fathers."

You calling me SELFISH?

When Gnome was about four-years-old, Tall Child had to hogtie his twisting body, routinely, to dress him. Gnome, at 38 inches and 31 pounds, could put up a surprisingly strong fight, like when small dogs and cats shock you with their belligerent force. He yelled at his daddy, "Put me back in my bed!"

The ever-indulgent and super-sensitive Tall Child yelled at me, "Can you help me out a little?" I played possum and enjoyed the audio.

I sympathized with Tall Child. No one wants to sweat through a physical struggle before 7:00 a.m., but Gnome couldn't reason yet. Man-handling was required. Tall Child was especially annoyed because I was on vacation. I slept in, and he took both boys to school. Once Tall Child safely deposited Sharky and Gnome, he called me and said, "You know, you could let Gnome sleep in late tomorrow or even stay home with you." Friends, sister-wives, mothers, *working* mothers, let me ask you this:

How often do you have a day off, at home, by yourself?

I told Tall Child, "No. I need a break from all children, including mine. I am not selfish. I am exhausted."

He then rattled off a list of things I "could do" while I was off. Women, when you have time off, do you make work lists for yourselves?

Stop. Drop. Roll onto the sofa. You deserve a break.

Ironically, when stop working these days, Tall Child often says, "Don't worry about those dishes. Come in here and relax for a minute." It's funny; the more I ask him to do, the more he seems to understand my fatigue.

Bags and I had this very conversation a few years ago. I accused Tall Child of leaving three times each morning, as in:

Door. "I forgot my check card." Door.

Door. "I left my phone." Door.

Door. "Have you seen my ...?" Door.

I told her that my coast wasn't clear until he passed the stop sign at the bottom of the neighborhood. We discussed the rare luxury of being home alone, and I asked, "Am I selfish?"

She exclaimed, "Are you kidding? No! When Guitar Hero leaves for work, I do snow angels in the bed!"

There are magic buttons in my house. One is in my favorite spot on the sofa. The moment my rear end meets cushion, a sound-alarm goes off. The other button is at the bottom step in our basement laundry room. Once my foot hits the floor, I hear,

"Mama!"

"Mama?"

"Somebody's calling your work phone & Gnome answered it!"

"Hey, Bug, can you help me...."

"I'm hungry."

"Where's the ....?"

"Where's Gnome?"

"Look what Gnome did!"

"Why didn't you buy groceries this week?"

"Uh-oh."

"How do you use a hammer?"

Sisters, do you fix a plate of food that you spent two hours cooking, and sit down to enjoy it, only to immediately set the plate aside and care for someone else? Spanx should have built-in springs.

So Tall Child laid down the working mama guilt gauntlet during that fall break. And, I caved. I let Gnome play hooky. I pitched a whiffle ball to him all morning in our backyard. We sat *inside* Chick-fil-A for lunch, and we picked Sharky up early from school. Reader, it was a good day.

I hope you found a friend on every page of this book. You'll enjoy the second of Theories, too! Find *Theories, Size 12: Volume DD* on Amazon.com, Kindle, retail bookstores, or on my website www.jodydyer.com. Theories include:

In the Christmas season men need to do as they are told.
Chunky girls need love songs, too.
Mama's behavior determines whether others like her baby.
Senior Superlatives must be modernized and include teachers.
Men are easier to work with than women.

***

Find all my work on Amazon and Kindle, or through my website, **www.jodydyer.com.** Want to be a part of the research? If so, friend and follow me on social media! I frequently ask readers for input. On Facebook: *Author Jody Dyer*

***

Interested in telling your own story?
I serve writers at all skill levels as a writing coach and editor. Contact me at dyer.cbpublishing@gmail.com for information.

Delicious's onion dip recipe. Whip this up when you're three sheets to the wind.

Ingredients: 1 packet of Lipton's dry onion soup mix.
              16 ounces of sour cream (real, not fat free)
Directions: Stir.

Pairs with Ruffles potato chips and alcohol and tastes better near moving water...like a river in the Great Smoky Mountains. Yee-haw!

www.ingramcontent.com/pod-product-compliance
Lightning Source LLC
Chambersburg PA
CBHW071204070526
44584CB00019B/2906